THE STATE
IN THE NEW TESTAMENT

THE STATE
in the
New Testament

by OSCAR CULLMANN

Dr. Theol., D.D. (*Edinburgh*);

D.D. (*Manchester*)

Professor in Basel and Paris

CHARLES SCRIBNER'S SONS

New York

[v]

Library of Congress Catalog Card Number 56-7123

Dedicated in Gratitude
to the Seminaries and Universities
in the United States
whose guest it was my privilege to be
from January to April, 1955

Foreword

INTEREST in the problem of Church and State usually becomes really vital only when open conflict between the
two arises. Thus it is no accident that in the years preced-
ing and during the last war an especially large number of
theological works were published on historical questions
concerning the attitude of the oldest Christian writings
toward the State.[1] Although no one will assert that since

---

[1] Among the many publications of these years I mention only the following: G. Dehn, *Engel und Obrigkeit, ein Beitrag zum Verständnis
von Römerbrief 13:1–7, Festschrift K. Barth,* 1936; K. L. Schmidt, *Das
Gegenüber von Kirche und Staat in der Gemeinde des Neuen Testaments, Theologische Blätter,* 1937, pp. 1ff; K. Barth, *Rechtfertigung
und Recht,* 1938; F. J. Leenhardt, *Le chrétien doit-il servir l'Etat?,*
1939; G. Kittel, *Christus und Imperator. Das Urteil der ersten
Christen über den Staat,* 1939; Otto Eck, *Urgemeinde und Imperium,*
1940; K. L. Schmidt, *Die Polis in Kirche und Welt. Eine lexikogra-
phische und exegetische Studie,* 1939; W. Bieder, *Ekklesia und Polis
im Neuen Testament und in der Alten Kirche,* 1941; O. Cullmann,
Königsherrschaft Christi und Kirche im Neuen Testament, 1941.

the war's end the problem of Church and State has lost
its burning contemporary relevance, it is the purpose of
the present work to show that this is by no means a problem connected only with particular historical crises, but
one which arises because of the very essence and presuppositions of the Christian faith. It is a problem which
exists also in countries and times in which there appears
to be no conflict at all. The following studies, therefore,
are intended to contribute not only to an understanding
of the life-and-death decisions modern Christians must or
may be called upon to make in desperate situations when
threatened by totalitarian governments or perhaps by certain forms of the Church with intolerable political ambi-
tions; they are intended also to indicate the equally real
and important responsibility of *every* Christian—also the
Christian living under so-called "normal," "everyday" conditions—to face and answer a serious problem which confronts him simply because he *is* a Christian.

I WISH to express my sincere thanks to the Hewett Lec-
tureship Foundation, through whose invitation I was
given the opportunity to read these lectures before atten-
tive and kindly appreciative audiences in Union Theological Seminary in New York, the Episcopal Theological
School in Cambridge and the Andover Newton Theological School. Grateful recognition is due also to the Rev-
erend Stuart D. Currie, who, during my stay in Emory
University in Georgia as guest professor, was of invaluable

help in the preparation of the English manuscript. His deep theological understanding greatly facilitated our work together.

OSCAR CULLMANN

Basel, Switzerland

March 15, 1956

Contents

xi

THE STATE
IN THE NEW TESTAMENT

Introduction: the Problem

THE New Testament cannot be used directly as a source for solving all our contemporary problems. There are some problems—that of the relation of Christianity towards culture, for instance—which can only be solved by indirect deduction from what the New Testament says.[1] There are other problems which are actually posed and solved by the New Testament. The question of Church and State is one of them: it is so closely bound up with the Gospel itself that they emerge together. The fundamental importance which this question has retained through successive generations until today was present from the very beginning.

The fact that the problem of Church and State is of such central importance is a corollary of the eschatological

[1] See *Het Oudste Christendom en de antieke Cultuur*, Vol. II, 1951, pp. 372ff.

attitude of Christianity. Because the Gospel presents itself as the "politeuma," the community of the coming age, it must accordingly see as its most intrinsic concern its disposition toward the present "polis," the secular State. Where the expectation of the end is taken seriously in Christianity, it becomes necessary to assume toward the earthly State an attitude based on principle—and yet not in such a way that the State as such would be renounced a priori.

It is really false to understand the Christian expectation of the end as if it were equivalent to indifference to present earthly values. On the contrary: from the Christian expectation of the end proceed very strong impulses toward dealings with the world. Christian eschatology does not mean simply "denial of the world," nor, to be sure, "affirmation of the world." We shall see at the end of these chapters that this complex situation—"neither affirmation nor denial of the world"—goes back to the chronological dualism which appears in primitive Christian conviction. This is the conviction that, on the one hand, in Christ the end is already fulfilled; and that nonetheless the consummation is still in the future, since the framework of the present world still endures.[2] We shall see that this dualism has already found expression in the primitive conception of the State.

The relationship of the Christian to the State is accordingly expressed first of all in temporal categories: the State

---

[2] This is the thesis I have developed in my book "Christ and Time." See especially ᴐp. 211ff.

appears as something "provisional." For this reason we do
not find anywhere in the New Testament a renunciation
of the State as such as a matter of principle; but neither
do we find an uncritical acceptance—as if the State itself
were something final, definitive.

The complex notion of the "provisional" character of
the State is the reason why the attitude of the first Christians toward the State is not unitary, but rather *appears* to
be contradictory. I emphasize, that it *appears* to be so. We
need only mention Romans 13:1, "Let every man be subject to the powers that be . . . ," alongside Revelation 13: the State as the beast from the abyss. In both
instances the *same* Roman State is spoken of. We shall see
that the true problem lies in this juxtaposition, which can be
traced throughout the whole New Testament. To explain
this juxtaposition is the purpose of these chapters.

The situation of the New Testament is not simple, but
complex. For that reason the New Testament problems also
are not simple but complex. They are not as simple as non-
theologians generally wish them to be. They admit that
philosophical problems are complex. But they wish the
theological problems to be quite simple and harmless.
However the theological reality is complex. Therefore we
have to *clarify*, not to simplify the problems.

In the course of this book we shall have to speak, on
the one hand, of a question of theoretical theology—that
is, the New Testament *doctrine* of the State—and at the
same time of the practical, dramatic tension between the
first Christians and the State. In this question, doctrine

and life are especially closely linked. The problem, "Gospel and State," belongs not only to the chapter, "The Doctrine of Jesus," but also to the chapter, "The Life of Jesus" —indeed, it belongs also to the most central point in the whole New Testament, the record of Jesus' death. If we were to forget this, we should find a forcible reminder in the inscription over the cross, which publishes the alleged offense for which Jesus was executed by the Romans: "King of the Jews." Translated into the legal parlance of the Roman State, this means: Jesus was condemned to death by hanging as a rebel against the Roman State in one of its subject provinces. In other words, he was nailed to the cross as a Zealot. Thus it becomes clear that the problem, "Church and State," is inherent in the New Testament. Rightly, therefore, the person of Pontius Pilate belongs somewhere in New Testament theology; and it is quite appropriate that he is mentioned very early in the short summaries of the Christian faith, and again later in the Old Roman formula, the precursor of our Apostles' Creed.[3]

Thus in the cross of Christ the relationship between "Christ and Caesar" stands at once in the beginning and at the center of the Christian faith. As a corollary, the problem, "Church and State," is posed for the Church at all times, forever: "For my sake you will be dragged before princes and kings, to bear witness before them and the gentiles" (Matt. 10:18). This does not mean that the Church must of necessity be persecuted by the State: it

[3] See O. Cullmann, *The Earliest Christian Confessions*, 1949, pp. 25ff.

does mean, however, that it must always reckon with the fact that it *can* be persecuted by the State. The cross of Christ should lead the Church in all its deliberations about the relationship of Church and State; not just in its negative aspects, but in its positive aspects as well. In the New Testament the cross has not yet become a religious symbol: it is a Roman sign of the most shameful death to modern sensibilities—the gallows. In this connection we must deal also with the judicial side of the trial of Jesus.

I. *Jesus and the Resistance Movement of the Zealots*

It is necessary, first of all, to see how the problem of the State presented itself to contemporary *Judaism*. The Jewish nation had lost its independence. To be sure, it possessed a certain autonomy within the framework of the Roman State. But the theocratic ideal, according to which the religious community, the Jewish "Congregation" (precursor of the Christian "Ecclesia"), coincided with the State, was realised only in scant measure. But first an observation is to be made here: an important distinction exists a priori, when one compares the attitude of Judaism toward the State with that of the Christian Church. In contemporary Judaism a *problem* of the State had existed long before there was a Christian problem of the State

To a superficial consideration, it might appear that in its relationship to the State Christianity simply took over the heritage of Judaism, and that the problem poses itself in exactly the same way here as there. Actually, however, the Jewish theocratic ideal is expressly rejected by Christianity as satanic—we need only recall the temptation stories in the Gospel. Satan offers to Christ the kingdoms of the world. Only to superficial consideration can it appear that the problem was the same merely because there was persecution of the Jews by the Roman State, just as there was persecution of the Christians by the Roman State. The time of the Maccabees is sometimes cited as a parallel. Yet the Christian resistance is to be judged quite otherwise, since it proceeds from an entirely different ideal. The Gospel knows nothing of that confusion of the Kingdom of God with the State which is characteristic of the theocratic ideal of Judaism. On the contrary, it opposed the theocratic ideal of Judaism with the same sharpness with which it resisted the totalitarian claims of the Roman State. Judaism was persecuted by the Roman State because it had a genuinely political theocratic program. But this does not hold true for Christianity at its origin.

As might be expected in view of the Christian's attitude of eschatological dualism (mentioned above), the disciple of Jesus had to fight on two fronts. For he had at the same time to refuse those who, like the Sadducees, assented without reservation to the Roman domination, surrendering all hope of the Kingdom of God. The Sadducees are indeed the collaborationists of that time. They

were agreeable to every excess of executive power on the
part of the Romans. Jesus and emergent Christianity never
joined in this unreserved submission to the Roman State
—a submission which was born of religious indifference
They had to come to terms with the Sadducees only indirectly, however, since these Sadducee collaborationists
had no genuinely religious, theological program, but only
a political one.

Much more important for emergent Christianity was
the contrasting Jewish solution, the theocratic; the confusion between the State and the Jewish congregation, as
it was pursued by the Pharisees. On the basis of this ideal
the Pharisees could oppose the Roman State only on purely
negative terms. In view of their theocratic ideal, they had
to renounce the State unreservedly. For the question before us, the extreme wing of the anti-Roman resistance
party is of especial interest. This consisted of the so-called
Zealots (from the Greek word *zēlos*, zeal). Here the theocratic ideal finds its sharpest expression. For its realisation the Zealots preached a holy war; and they not only
preached it: they secretly prepared for it, menacing the
Roman garrison by individual resistance-actions and up-
risings, until in the years sixty through seventy A. D. it
came to the open war which ended with the destruction of
the Temple at Jerusalem by the Romans and the bloody
suppression of the Jewish resistance. The Zealots, however, did not disappear. Their party lived on, and sixty-
five years later, under Hadrian, a second war occurred in
which Barkochba, the commander of the resistance

troops, had himself proclaimed Messiah and political king over Israel. This second insurrection ended with the final annihilation of the Jewish national existence. Recently this second war has been drawn to our attention in an astonishing way by the sensational discovery (at Murabba'at) of two documents. In that same region around the Dead Sea in which the text-rolls of the important sect of the Essenes were found, two original manuscripts of the Messiah-king Barkochba to one of his officers came to light. Those caves, which had once hidden old manuscripts, obviously served also, in the second Jewish war, as "Maquis"—that is, hiding places—for the insurrectionists.[1] But our present interest centers primarily in the first war, and particularly in the revolutionary movements which led up to it.

For the understanding of the New Testament and of the events which led up to the death of Jesus, the Zealot movement is of extraordinary significance. Certainly it is an exaggeration to make Jesus himself a Zealot—an excess connected with the name of R. Eisler [2]—but I shall try to show that it is also an error to underestimate the importance of the Zealots for the doctrine and life of primitive Christianity, and for its conception of the State.[3] Above all, we must not overlook the fact that *Jesus was con-*

---

[1] See R. de Vaux, *Quelques textes hebreux de Murabba'at* (*Revue biblique* 1953, pp. 268ff); J. T. Milik, *Une lettre de Simeon Bar Kokheba* (*Revue biblique* 1953, pp. 276ff).

[2] R. Eisler, Ἰησοῦς βασιλεὺς οὐ βασιλεύσας, 2 vol. 1929/30, id. *The Messiah Jesus and John the Baptist*, 1931.

[3] S. G. F. Brandon, *The Fall of Jerusalem and the Christian Church*, 1951, has rightly emphasized this importance.

demned to death on the cross by the Romans as a Zealot.
In our next chapter we shall speak of this in greater
detail. The bare fact must be mentioned here as sufficient
indication in itself of the importance of the Zealot movement for our problem. As seen by the Roman officials, the
"Case of Jesus of Nazareth" belonged in the long list of
cases of Zealots, arrested for offenses against the Roman
State in its Jewish provinces, who had to be rendered
harmless. It is true that we shall see this judgment led
to injustice; for Jesus was not a Zealot. But it is also true
that he had to come to terms with this movement at every
step of the way, and to explain his relationship to it. That
we have to do here with one of the questions which most
strongly engaged the attention of every mind in Palestine,
is no indirect conclusion. Rather shall we see that Jesus
had with him in his innermost circle of disciples Zealots—
or at least former Zealots. We shall see that he obviously
exercised a special power of attraction over these people;
and, on the other hand, that he was continually forced to
distinguish his own preaching from theirs.

Thanks to Josephus, we are rather well informed on
these insurrection movements of the Zealots. He speaks
of them again and again both in the *Bellum Judaicum*
(especially in the second book) and in the *Antiquities*
(especially in books eighteen and twenty).[4] An insurrection led by the Zealot Judas of Gamala obviously excited

---

[4] Concerning the zealots in Josephus see E. Schürer, *Geschichte des
jüdischen Volkes im Zeitalter Jesu Christi*, 4th ed., Vol. I, 1901, pp.
573ff, 617ff. Also A. Schlatter, *Geschichte Israels von Alexander dem
Grossen bis Hadrian*, 1925, pp. 322ff.

a special sensation. This outbreak occurred at the beginning of the first century after Christ in connection with a
property assessment, and was quelled with much bloodshed by the Romans.[5] The event was long held in remembrance by the Jews. In Acts 5:36, 37 this Judas is mentioned by Gamaliel in connection with another Zealot
leader named Theüdas. By this the author of Acts is led
into a chronological error, into which we need not go here.
I mention the passage only to show how much in the
foreground of interest the Zealot question stood in New
Testament times.[6] It is also important to emphasise here
that, in the passage from Acts just cited, Gamaliel places
Jesus in the same category with those leaders of the
Zealots. Thus to outsiders, at least, Jesus and the Zealot
leaders appeared to have something in common. According to Acts 21:38, the Roman tribune before whom Paul
was haled considered him a Zealot. In fact he thinks Paul
may be the Egyptian Zealot leader whose insurrection is
also recorded by Josephus. "Are you not the Egyptian who
has caused an insurrection of 4000 Zealots?" [7] This shows
once again to what an extraordinary extent the Roman garrison was obsessed by the thought of the Zealots—today we
would say the garrison suffered from a persecution complex!
Everywhere the zealotism of the Jews gave the Romans

[5] Josephus, *Antiquitates judaicae,* XVIII, 1:1ff; XX, 5:2ff; *De bello
judaico,* II, 8:1, 17:8; VII, 8:1.
[6] In contradiction to the description of Josephus, F. J. Foakes-Jackson
and Kirsopp Lake, *The Beginnings of Christianity* (Vol. I, 1920, pp.
421ff), dispute Judas' belonging to the zealot movement, and attempt
to fix the beginning of the movement much later.
[7] *Bell. jud.,* II, 13:5; *Ant.* XX, 8:6.

the jitters. In the passage named above (Acts 21:38)—
and it appears elsewhere as well—we find the Romans'
Latin designation for the Zealots: "sicarii" [8] (literally, cut-
throats, bandits). From the Roman point of view, they
were anarchists.

Quite likely the "Galileans" mentioned by Jesus in Luke
13:1 are to be equated with the Zealots. We read here:
Someone informs Jesus of "the Galileans whose blood
Pilate had mingled with their sacrifices." I do not believe
we have to do here with a slaughter in the Temple, as
some have assumed. Josephus, at any rate, knows nothing
of such an event. By "sacrifices" men must be intended.
Probably we have to do here with a Zealot uprising in
which some Romans, or at least officials of the State, lost
their lives. Pilate may have availed himself of the opportunity of launching a blood-bath among all the Galilean
Zealots who were within reach when opportunity presented itself. It is worthy of notice that this event was
reported precisely to Jesus. Obviously it was assumed
that he took special interest in these people.

This assumption was supported by the fact that Jesus
had Zealots around him in his inner circle of disciples.
How do we know this? We can say with certainty that
one member of the group of twelve chosen disciples belonged to the Zealots—or at least had belonged to them
before his calling. In the list of disciples found in chapter
six of Luke's Gospel, and in the list in Acts 1, which sub-
stantially agrees with Luke, he is named Simon the Zealot.

[8] *Ant.*, XX, 8:10.

This is the same person who is designated Simon "ho kananaios" in the parallel lists of Mark (3:18) and Matthew (10:4). These words are always mistranslated as "Simon the Canaanite" (that is, from Canaan). Actually, however, *kananaios* has nothing whatever to do with the land of Canaan. It is simply a transcription of the Aramaic designation for Zealots. Zealot is the Greek word, from zēlos, zeal. The Zealots are the zealous. Kananaios comes from the Semitic noun "Kana," zeal. Kenana is the Aramaic word for Zealot, just as sicarius is the Latin word for the same member of the Jewish resistance party.

It is quite possible, moreover, that still others of the Twelve were Zealots, or former Zealots. The name of Judas Iscariot has still not been satisfactorily explained. The Codex Sinaiticus at John 6:71 dissects Iscariot into ish Kariot; that is, man from Kerioth. But we know of no place by this name. We may therefore quite properly consider whether Iscariot may not be a Semitic transcription of the Latin word "sicarius." (Cf. the reading *Skariōth*, found in Codex Bezae and the Itala.) Philologically it is quite probable. If Judas was a member of the Zealot party, then we can understand his betrayal much more simply. For he would then have had a messianic ideal quite different from Jesus'; and his entry into the circle of disciples would have rested on a misapprehension of the goal Jesus was pursuing. Like others of the disciples, he would have pictured Jesus' role as something quite different: namely, as that of a messiah-king, after the pattern of Judas of Gamala and the later Barkochba: a king who would bring the Roman rule to an end and thus establish the kingdom of God on earth. On this view, Judas' betrayal would stem from a disillusionment which the other disciples also experienced when they saw that Jesus conceived his messianic role quite differently, defining as satanic that political messianic hope which was the highest ideal of the Zealots.

We must inquire further, whether Peter is not to be named in this connection also. Peter it is who wants to restrain Jesus from fulfilling his task as Messiah in suffering rather than in earthly lordship; and it is Peter whom Jesus must rebuke with the words, "Get thee behind me, Satan!" For Jesus recognises that the same tempter confronts him here; just as in the Temptations proper, where (according to Luke's and Matthew's account) the devil offered him world dominion. The Johannine Gospel indicates that Peter had a sword with him in Gethsemane, and was obviously quite willing to use it after the fashion of the sicarii. In addition, there is a philological consideration which makes at least probable the hypothesis that Peter belonged to the Zealots. In my book on Peter,[9] I have indicated that the designation "Bar Jona," applied to Peter in Matthew 16:17, cannot with absolute certainty be translated "son of John." To be sure, it is thus construed in John 1:42 and 21:15. But this may well be a secondary explanation, for there is no documentary evidence for Jona as an abbreviation for Joḥanan. Following R. Eis-

[9] P. 16.

ler [10] I have mentioned in my book that according to an old Hebrew lexicon (cited by G. Dalman) [11] *barjona* is a word borrowed from Accadian, meaning "terrorist." Thus we would have here yet another designation for Zealot.

Finally we may raise the question, whether the sons of Zebedee do not exhibit tendencies associated with the Zealot movement. In Mark 10:37 we read their request to be allowed to sit on the right and left hand of Jesus when he is enthroned in glory as king of the world. This is a typically Zealot request. Their attitude in Luke 9:54 points in the same direction. When the Samaritans refuse to receive Jesus, the sons of Zebedee want fire called down from heaven to destroy them; and they have to be rebuked by Jesus. The nickname "sons of thunder" given them by Jesus is further evidence that they had Zealot tendencies. We may therefore conclude: One of the Twelve—Simon the Zealot—*certainly* belonged to the Zealots; others *probably* did, like Judas Iscariot, Peter, and *possibly* the sons of Zebedee.

Jesus must have had an especially strong attraction for these people, so we can readily understand that he had to come to terms almost daily with the Zealot question. We can also understand that for Jesus the Zealot ideal constituted the true temptation—from the very beginning, when the devil offered him world dominion after

[10] *Op. cit.*, p. 67.
[11] G. Dalman, *Aramäisch-neuhebräisches Wörterbuch*, 2nd ed., 1922, 65a.

his baptism, to the moment when he rebuked Peter as Satan, and finally to the decisive moment in Gethsemane, when the devil once again tempted him in the same way as in the beginning—as the Gospel of Luke accurately interprets (Chapter 4:13): "When the devil had ended all the temptation, he departed from him until another occasion." There in Gethsemane for the last time the question is posed, whether Jesus will yield to the pressure of his disciples and offer resistance to the Roman soldiers who have come to arrest him. At the end of the prayer Jesus is satisfied: he is inalterably determined to finish his course, fulfilling *his* messianic calling, as the suffering Son of Man.

Peter's denial does not take place until he sees that Jesus will not defend himself. It may indeed be attributable to Peter's human weakness—but, like Judas' betrayal, it surely rests on a final disillusionment as well.

When we speak of Jesus' attitude toward the State we need not, as is usually stated, limit ourselves to the saying about tax-paying in Mark 12:13ff. On the contrary, we must start from Jesus' attitude toward the Zealots.

Above all, we insist that in Jesus as in the whole New Testament we find in their criticism of the State that duality of which we spoke at the start. On the one hand, we see that he certainly does not regard the State as in any sense a *final*, divine institution: on the other hand, we see that he accepts the State and radically renounces every attempt to overthrow it. In this book I wish to emphasise that this double attitude is characteristic of the entire New Testament, and to show that it roots in a basic conception which is thoroughly unitary. And it is important to see that already in Jesus we find this attitude toward the State—double indeed, but *not* contradictory.

First Jesus' critical attitude. He did not accept the State as a final institution. This is evident from certain sayings which do not indicate any particular respect for the rulers. In Luke 13:32 when he observes that Herod, the ruler appointed by the Romans, wants to run him out of his territory with a threat, he does not hesitate to call that official a "fox." In Luke 22:25, with that characteristic irony he so often used, Jesus speaks of the rulers' custom of adorning themselves with the honorific title, "benefactor"—this was done, incidentally, on coins. They rule, says Jesus, by the use of force, oppressing the people, and still call themselves "benefactors."

One could also point out that Jesus accepted the classification of the hated tax-collectors as "collaborationists" —a classification customary among the Pharisees and especially among the people. He names the tax-collectors in the same breath with sinners, prostitutes, and the heathen (Matt. 9:10; 18:17; 21:31).

On the other hand, however, we see that Jesus received the tax-collectors and sinners. Among the Twelve are numbered not only Zealots, but a tax-collector as well (Mark 2:15, Matt. 9:10; 10:3). Greater enemies than Zealots and tax-collectors cannot be imagined. The fact that Jesus called tax-collectors along with Zealots shows bet-

ter than anything else that he stood beyond this opposition.

Jesus' attitude both toward the tax-collectors and toward the centurion from Capernaum must have dis-
pleased the Zealots, in spite of whatever sympathy his
inner independence of Herod could inspire in them.

We turn now to another question: Are there among the
sayings of Jesus some which apply directly to the Zealots
and their endeavors? There are indeed; and their number
is singularly great. Bearing in mind the importance of
the Zealot question in Jesus' time, we assert that sayings
otherwise hard to understand make sense only when they
are referred to the Zealots. It has long been recognised
that only in connection with the Zealot movement can
one understand Jesus' celebrated response: "Render unto
Caesar the things that are Caesar's; and to God the things
that are God's" (Mark 12:17, and parallels).

But I believe many other sayings belong in this category as well. Special light is cast on the injunction in the
Sermon on the Mount, "not to resist one who is evil,"
when we consider that Jesus had to discuss continually
the ideal of the Zealots, who wanted to resist the Roman
State by force of arms. But I call particular attention here
to the difficult saying about those "who offer violence to
the Kingdom of God, the violent who seize it by force"
(Matt. 11:12. Cf. Luke 16:16). It has long been a matter
of vigorous controversy, whether this saying is to be construed "in bonam partem" or "in malam partem"—
whether it contains praise or censure. Is the intention

here to praise zeal for the Kingdom of God? Is indeed
Jesus himself, as Albert Schweitzer thinks, to be reckoned
among those who fought so impetuously to gain the Kingdom of God? I do not think the Greek expression will allow this interpretation. Much rather are we to think of
people like the Zealot leader Judas.[12] To be sure, the saying has more in it than just blame alone. Jesus recognised
that these people were concerned about the Kingdom of
God. But he nevertheless renounced their action, because
the Kingdom of God is not brought in by human power,
nor is it set up as a political kingdom. Once again we ascertain that this duality is present in Jesus himself. Surely
the Kingdom of God should be of infinitely more value to
us than the State; but it is wrong to attack the State vio-
lently in order to set up the Kingdom of God. Among the
"violent" belong also those in John 6:15 who wanted to
make Jesus king, and from whom Jesus withdrew. Is the
saying in the Sermon on the Mount (Matt. 7:15) about
the false prophets who "come in sheep's clothing but in-
wardly are ravenous wolves" directed against the Zealots?
One cannot say with certainty; but the question may be
raised.

The tenth chapter of the Johannine Gospel, with its
discussion of the true shepherd, contains, it seems to me,
what must be regarded as in some sense an interpretation of the saying found in Matthew 11:12, about those

---

[12] So also A. von Gall, βασιλεία τοῦ θεοῦ, 1926, p. 353, and already H.
Windisch, *Der messianische Krieg und das Urchristentum*, 1909, pp.
35f.

who seize the Kingdom of God by force. In John 10:8 the Johannine Christ makes the strange statement: "All who came before me are thieves and robbers." In verse 11 the true shepherd is contrasted with them—the shepherd who saves the life of the sheep. The false shepherds do not spare the life of the sheep. Are not the Zealot leaders in mind here, who led their followers to certain death at the hands of the Romans? It is impossible to think of the prophets or John the Baptist as among the thieves and robbers.[13] It seems to me all but certain that the Zealot leaders like Judas of Gamala are in mind here. It is also noteworthy that Jesus is compared to them. Seen from the outside, there must have been something common to both. The radical distinction is expressed a few verses later: "No man taketh my life from me; but I lay it down of myself" (v. 18).

This brings us to the subject of the second chapter: Jesus' Condemnation by the Romans. We shall see that Jesus was in fact condemned by the Romans as a Zealot like the Zealots before him. To see how this accusation became possible even though Jesus consciously dissociated himself from the Zealots, we shall have first of all to explore further sayings of Jesus. And we shall see even more

[13] Certainly the Pharisees are not meant thereby as A. Schlatter maintains in his *Der Evangelist Johannes*, 1930, *ad. loc.* But on the other hand, nothing indicates that we should think of "revealers and saviours of the Hellenistic-Gnostic world" as Bultmann maintains in his *Das Evangelium des Johannes*, 1941, *ad. loc.* In the footnote on p. 289 (number 2) Bultmann admits, however, that one could think of political saviours "in so far as they are religious, that is, pseudo-messianic." This is a valid description of the zealot leaders.

clearly that the key to understanding is furnished by the fact asserted here; that Jesus' attitude is to be sought beyond any uncritical absolutising of the Roman State, and at the same time beyond any thoroughgoing political resistance to it.

II.   *Jesus' Condemnation by the Roman State*

WE HAVE seen that Jesus had Zealots around him in his closest company; that he obviously exercised an exceptional power of attraction over the partisans of this resistance movement; that seen from without, his appearance with his disciples could have been mistaken for Zealotism; and that from the beginning Jesus set himself at a distance from the Zealots in a variety of ways, in order to prevent the diversion of his work onto a false track.

Christ regarded as expressly satanic the understanding of the Messiah which was advocated by the Zealots and which involved a confusion of the Kingdom of God with an earthly form of the State aimed at world domination. And truly one is tempted only by the things which stand near him.

Thus the question of messianic consciousness is raised.
We cannot deal here with this question in all its complexity; we wish only to indicate the point which is basic
to the understanding both of Jesus' attitude and also of
his condemnation: namely, that Jesus regarded himself as
the Son of Man who would one day come on the clouds
of heaven. This Son of Man who is treated of in the book
of Daniel and in the more or less esoteric Jewish writings
of the first century is, however, a messianic figure. To be
sure, the genuine Jewish Messiah is a victorious national
commander-in-chief who conquers all heathen peoples
and rules over the world; whereas the Danielic Son of
Man comes from heaven and establishes a kingdom which
is not of this world. But the connections between Messiah
and Son of Man are of such a sort that we can properly
speak of Jesus' messianic consciousness. Jesus was conscious of being the divine emissary, sent to establish the
Kingdom of God. Only thus do we understand how Jesus
became liable to the indictment which ended in his condemnation, the grounds for which were posted publicly
on the cross. Jesus' guilt, from the Roman point of view,
consisted in this: that—just like the Zealots—he was pre-
sumed to have aimed at kingly authority in one of the subject provinces of the Romans. Jesus' condemnation by the
Romans (and we shall see that from the legal standpoint
it was actually by the Romans, not by the Jews, that Jesus
was condemned), his condemnation would be incompre-
hensible if Jesus had not in fact regarded himself as the
Son of Man who came to establish the Kingdom of God

in the world. To me this is the strongest evidence of what
we call Jesus' self-consciousness.

But it is a fact deserving special notice that, in order
to explain his divinely appointed task, Jesus intentionally
applied to himself the Jewish conception of the "Son of
Man," and not that of the political Messiah. It is quite true
that he never directly refused the title Messiah; yet he
always displayed a quite determined restraint as soon as
he was called Messiah. He did not want it discussed; and
as soon as anyone called him Messiah he commanded him
to be silent. W. Wrede, as we know, has designated this
command to silence as a later invention of the Evangelists.[1] By this so-called "Messianic secret" Mark is sup-
posed to have wanted to explain how it happened that
Jesus was not recognised during his lifetime. I consider
this interpretation entirely unnecessary, and believe that
the command to silence has its basis in the actual interpretation which Jesus in fact placed upon his messianic
calling. Only his distinctive sense of mission will suffice to
explain Jesus' command to silence and his pronounced restraint at the title of Messiah.

In the decisive moments of his life when he was asked
whether he was the Messiah, Jesus quite characteristically
never answered the question with a 'yes'; but on every
occasion returned an answer which intentionally avoided
that title and replaced it with the other title: "the Son of
Man." This was the case in Caesarea Philippi (Mark
8:29) when Jesus asked the disciples, "And you, who do

[1] W. Wrede, *Das Messiasgeheimnis in den Evangelien,* 1901.

you say that I am?" and Peter answered, "You are the Messiah." Jesus responded to this so-called confession neither with 'yes' nor with 'no,' but enjoined silence. He himself proceeds, however (v. 31), teaching that the *Son of Man* "must suffer many things." Thus he does not say the *Messiah* must suffer many things, but rather the "Son of Man." The Evangelist has preserved the recollection that Jesus did not apply the title Messiah to himself, because it was too heavily weighted with the ideal of political kingship and could lead to Zealot misunderstandings. When Peter, on this same occasion, took Jesus aside and tried to restrain him from construing his calling as that of God's Suffering Servant, Jesus recognised that the same temptation faced him as had confronted him already at the beginning of his public ministry: to establish an earthly Kingdom of God! Jesus observes that it is the same devil, this time making use of Peter. This proves that, according to Mark (we are not speaking here of the parallel text, Matt. 16) Peter held the Zealot interpretation of the Messiah, when he said; "You are the Messiah." Jesus regarded this interpretation as satanic: "Get thee behind me, Satan!" (v. 33).[2]

We find the same attitude later on, moreover, in Jesus' hearing before the high priest. We shall see subsequently that the intention of this hearing was not to arrive at a *judicial verdict*, but to lay the foundation for a denunciation of Jesus to the *Romans* on the part of the Jews. For

[2] For further details on this point and on the connection between this text and Matt. 16:16ff, see O. Cullmann, *Peter*, 1952, pp. 170ff.

the high priest knew that the Romans were interested only in messianic pretensions; because Messiah meant to them what it actually was for the Zealots: namely, a revolutionary pretender to the Jewish royal throne. Therefore the high priest puts the question (Mark 14:61 and parallels): "Are you the Messiah?" He presumably expected an affirmative answer. At the same time, however, a negative answer—a possibility which had to be considered—would not have been unfavorable to the high priest's cause, since Jesus would have been so discredited in the eyes of that segment of the population enlisted in the Zealot movement that in their disillusionment those followers of Jesus who had been drawn from or influenced by the Zealots would have left him in the lurch. As so often occurred, the occasion presented itself to Jesus to compromise himself. But as he did just as often in such situations, Jesus refused to compromise himself. For just as in the case of the question about taxpaying, he answered neither 'yes' nor 'no.' According to Mark, it is true, the answer might have been "yes"; "I am." But when we compare the text of Matthew and of Luke we are obliged to question whether Mark has rightly understood the Aramaic words here. In Matthew these Aramaic words appear to be quite literally translated into Greek: "You say so," whereby the "you" is emphasised. Now the orientalists are agreed that the corresponding Aramaic words, "*you* say so" do not mean a clear 'yes' in this language, but rather are a means of evading the question, and indeed can occasionally even mean 'no.' They are used,

then, in the following sense: "That is what *you* say, not
I." Here too, moreover, as in Caesarea Philippi Jesus proceeds in the next sentence with a statement once again
not about the Messiah but about the *Son of Man: "On the
contrary* [3] I tell you, hereafter you will see the Son of
Man," etc. The parallel Lukan text confirms the fact that
Jesus did not answer the high priest's question with a
'yes,' because he knew the title Messiah was liable to misunderstanding. Here in chapter 22:67ff we read: "If I tell
you, you will not believe; and if I ask you, you will not
answer. But from now on the Son of Man shall be seated
at the right hand of the power of God." Luke has rightly
understood the Aramaic words to this effect: that Jesus
evaded the question: that on no occasion did he designate
himself as the Messiah, so that no support could be found
in such a declaration for the accusation that he was a
Zealot. On the other hand, it is true, he did not disavow
his consciousness of mission, since he did in fact designate
himself as the heavenly Son of Man, who as such had no
political program. [4]

The third place is Mark 15:2 with its parallels. Here
Jesus is standing before Pilate. Pilate asks him: "Are you
the King of the Jews?" Here the connection with the
Zealot indictment is clear. The Roman official, of course,

---

[3] In Greek πλήν expressing a strong contrast.

[4] I shall give detailed proof of the interpretation represented here in my
Christology of the New Testament, which will soon be published. See
also A. Merx, *Die vier kanonischen Evangelien,* Vol. II/1, 1902, pp.
382ff; Vol. II/2, p. 161. Further, J. Héring, *Le Royaume de Dieu et
sa venue,* 1937, pp. 111ff.

did not know the religious idea of the Messiah. In this instance Jesus' answer reads the same in all three Evangelists: *You* say so. It is probable that here too the evangelists understood this to mean 'yes.' But in view of the
Aramaic an evasive answer is a possibility. In any case,
we must consider the Fourth Evangelist, who, as we shall
establish later, precisely in the passion narrative, worked
in part with better traditions. He preserves the recollection that it was precisely before Pilate that Jesus emphasised the non-political nature of his calling. That is the
meaning of the dialogue in John 18:33ff about the kingdom which "is not of this world." At any rate it is remarkable that even in Mark 15:2 and parallels Pilate shows no
reaction whatever to Jesus' answer, "*You* say so." And a
reaction must surely have taken place if Pilate had inferred an affirmative answer from Jesus' reply to the question about kingship. We shall return to this point later.
Here it is sufficient to indicate that from the beginning of
his public ministry until its decisive close Jesus consist-
ently regarded the Zealot—that is, political—interpretation of the Messiah as a satanic temptation, and consequently combatted it. This temptation presented itself to
him for the first time immediately after his baptism.
Therefore all three synoptics connect Jesus' baptism with
the temptation. If my own explanation of the baptism
story is correct,[5] then it was precisely there that Jesus was
assigned the commission to undertake the role of God's
Suffering Servant; and then it is no accident that im-

[5] *Baptism in the New Testament*, 1950, pp. 16ff.

mediately thereafter he is confronted by the satanic temptation to be the sort of Messiah the Zealots had in mind
—a political ruler.

Yet was there not at least one moment when Jesus
yielded to the temptation? Do we not have in Luke
22:35ff at least *one* saying of Jesus which clearly com-
mands the disciples to fight with the sword after the manner of the Zealots? "Whoever has no sword, let him sell his
mantle and buy a sword." Some New Testament scholars
have maintained this. They say, to be sure, that Jesus
quickly recognised this avenue for a wrong turning.
Others—Robert Eisler above all—who go so far as to
make Jesus a Zealot, completely misunderstanding his
actual attitude, find their chief support in this saying,
which they interpret quite in accordance with the thinking of the Zealots. We must take a closer look at this saying.[6] In the passion narrative in Luke it stands immediately before the account of the arrest of Jesus in Gethsemane: "He said to them: I sent you forth without purse,
without bag or sandals. Did you lack anything? They answered: No, nothing. Then he said to them: But now let
him who has a purse take it with him, and likewise him
who has a bag. And whoever has no sword, let him sell his
mantle and buy a sword. For I tell you this which was
written must be fulfilled in me: He was reckoned among
the transgressors. As for me, thus does it come to pass.
Then they said: See, Lord, here are two swords. But he

[6] The different explanations are collected by E. Klostermann, *Das
Lukasevangelium*, 1929, *ad. loc.*

said: That is enough." How is this saying to be explained?

It is a fact that in Gethsemane at least one of those at Jesus' side (according to Luke, more than one) wore a sword; and this appears to substantiate Eisler's thesis. But according to Matthew it is just there that Jesus utters the saying which condemns all Zealotism: "All who take the sword shall perish by the sword" (Matt. 26:52). Should we not, then, understand figuratively the saying read above about the sword which the disciples are to buy? There are, to be sure, other sayings where Jesus spoke of the sword quite figuratively. This is true of Matthew 10:34, where he says: "I am come not to bring peace, but the sword." Here the allusion is to the persecution to which every disciple will be exposed. Nevertheless in our Lukan saying we must understand the word "sword" literally. For it is in fact grouped with such concrete things as purses, bags, and clothing. Here then Jesus really commanded his disciples to take a sword with them. We know that the context of Jesus' sayings has been lost and that the Evangelists, each in his own way, have constructed their own framework. It is therefore not absolutely certain that the saying belongs in the passion narrative where Luke has put it. Still it is most appropriate precisely at this time, when Jesus anticipates his death in the immediate future. Jesus knew that the death which was about to befall him would mean persecution for his followers. And yet they are to proclaim the Gospel. It is for their defense that they are to be equipped with a sword at this time. If we regard the saying as genuine (and I hold it impossible to assail its authenticity),[7] then we must in consequence take this command seriously. Even so I do not believe we may draw the conclusion that Jesus really embraced Zealotism here, even for a moment. I much rather believe that we find here in Jesus the same *tension* which is characteristic of his attitude toward the Roman State. His bearing can be described neither as simply assent nor as refusal.[8] He reckons with eventualities in which, for the sake of the proclamation of the Gospel, defensive sword-bearing may become a necessity for the disciples.

But the end of the conversation proves that Jesus did not thereby embrace Zealotism. The disciples say in their zeal: "Here are two swords!" Jesus observes that they have misunderstood his saying as Zealotism, as meaning an attack upon the Romans. Thereupon he breaks off the conversation abruptly, just as he does whenever anyone attributed the Messiah title to him. Thus he says here: "That is enough!" He observes that once again he has been misunderstood by his own followers, his words being taken in a political sense. So he prefers not to speak of the matter any further. That the Greek words are to be understood here in this sense seems to me proven precisely by Jesus' reaction in this same Gospel of Luke a few verses on, when his followers say: "Shall we strike with the sword?" After one of these men, who is almost certainly to

[7] H. Windisch, *Der messianische Krieg und das Urchristentum,* 1909, p. 48, places, certainly incorrectly, a question mark here.
[8] It seems to me that S. G. F. Brandon also disregards this in his *The Fall of Jerusalem and the Christian Church,* 1951.

be reckoned among the Zealots, has actually drawn his
sword, Jesus says in v. 51: "Thus far! No farther!" This
exclamation is exactly parallel to the "That is enough!"
in v. 38. Both warnings can be regarded as *characteristic
expressions* of Jesus' attitude toward the Zealots, as expressions of what I have called the "tension." Not everything in the Zealots' resistance is condemned. But there
is a limit which may not be transgressed. It is at the exact
point where Zealotism becomes a purely political, military
movement, and diverts his disciples from that task which
Jesus assigned to them: the proclamation of the Kingdom
of God. As disciples of Jesus they have to take a stand on
all questions, even political questions; but they do not
have to wage war *on their own initiative.* This is the limit
to their sword-bearing: "That is enough!"; "Thus far!"

Luke is probably right also in bringing the saying
about taxpaying into direct connection with the trial and
condemnation of Jesus. In Luke 23:2 we hear that the
Jews brought Jesus before Pilate with this accusation:
"We found this man inciting our people and forbidding
them to pay tribute to Caesar." This means, in other
words, he is a leader of the Zealots. The fact that it was
possible intentionally to misinterpret Jesus' saying (Mark
12:13) in this way proves that Jesus' answer was complex.

We know that it was just this question of *taxpaying*
which was regarded by the Zealots as the criterion, so to
speak, of loyalty to Judaism. As a matter of fact this very
question was indeed addressed to Jesus in order to "en-
trap him in his talk" (Mark 12:13). According to Mark,

it is the Pharisees and the Herodians who pose the question. Both groups are at one in wanting Jesus disarmed. And this is the only thing they have in common, for in other matters they are radically opposed. The question is: "Should we pay tribute to Caesar or not?" For themselves, the Pharisees would prefer to answer in the negative, although they do not, like the Zealots, draw the extreme consequences. The Herodians, on the contrary, are the collaborationists who make common cause with the Romans and naturally for themselves return an affirmative answer. It is just the presence of *both* groups which constitutes for Jesus the special temptation. Both want him to compromise himself. If he answers yes, he will be shown up as a collaborationist and will disillusion the majority of the people; for it is precisely in this connection that these have rested such great hope in him. If he answers no, this is an avowal that he himself is a Zealot, and indeed a leader of the Zealots; and we know what that meant to the Romans.

But Jesus does not so compromise himself. It is true that his answer has often been thus misconstrued, as if the sphere of Caesar is here presented as being *of equal value* with the sphere of God. But this is precisely *not* the case. If Jesus had really attributed to Caesar's sphere the same value as God's, then he would have placed himself on the side of the Herodians. For this is exactly what the collaborationists maintained: Caesar is God's counterpart. Actually Jesus does not say this. He merely recognises that within its sphere the State can demand what belongs to it: money, taxes. But it is not placed on the same level as God. Give God what is his! That means: your life, your entire person.

As in so many of Jesus' sayings, there is irony in this expression also. We must recall what Jesus says in another place about God and mammon. Give the mammon to Caesar. The Greek verb [9] even implies: give it *back*. The mammon belongs to Caesar: he has had his likeness impressed upon it. So let him have it! But return to God that which is *his* property, what he has given to us. That means: everything, body and soul. Here there can be no talk at all of equality between Caesar and God. The State is nothing final. But it may levy taxes. People should pay these even if it is to the heathen Roman State which has no proper right to the possession of Palestine.[10] Again, in Matthew 17:25 Jesus says that the kings of the earth exact custom and tribute from *aliens*. His disciples should not, therefore, waste their time and energy in resisting the payment of taxes—that is, against the existence of the Roman occupation forces—so long as it is merely a question of taxpaying, of money which indeed belongs to Caesar. But the saying Mark 12:13 has implicit in it this further purport: do not give Caesar *more* than his due! Give him nothing that belongs to God!

[9] ἀπόδοτε.

[10] A quite different interpretation is given by S. Kennard, *Render to God,* 1950. According to him the command to pay taxes is directed only to the collaborationists serving the Roman State. Concerning the monetary system of the time and its significance for the interpretation of this passage, see E. Stauffer, *Christus und die Caesaren,* 1946, p. 118ff.

Thus Jesus' whole position toward the State is clearly circumscribed, precisely in the duality it entails throughout. On the one hand, the State is nothing final. On the other, it has the right to demand what is necessary to its existence—but no more. Every totalitarian claim of the State is thereby disallowed. And the double imperative logically follows: on the one hand, do not let the Zealots draw you into a purely political martial action against the existence of the Roman State; on the other, do not give to the State what belongs to God! In the background we hear the challenge: if ever the State demands what belongs to God, if ever it hinders you in the proclamation of the Kingdom of God, then resist it. The whole *leitmotiv* of the complex New Testament attitude toward the State Jesus formulates here, in this saying.

Jesus did not allow himself to be entrapped here; and yet it is probably true, as Luke states, that the Jews, in denouncing him to the Romans, said that he incited the people not to pay taxes. Because Jesus' position on this question was not simple but *had* to be complex, men could mischievously distort his point of view, and they certainly did. Thus they distorted also his critical attitude toward the temple, representing it as a revolutionary intention to destroy it.

We must also take into account the fact that Jesus' twofold attitude toward the State and toward the Zealots was really misunderstood. We know that his own disciples did not understand it. Possibly they had already interpreted his entry into Jerusalem as his conscious seeking of a demonstration of political messianism. There are also modern historians who impute this meaning to Jesus' entry on Palm Sunday. Everything we have heard of Jesus' judgment upon the Zealots speaks against the view that he himself sought such a demonstration on Palm Sunday. The fact that he rode in on a donkey and not as a warlike Messiah on a horse—as he is described in Zechariah 9:9—could speak against a revolutionary intention. But it is certain that among the people and even among the disciples the entry itself was understood as a decisive act aimed at the establishment of the Kingdom of God within a national framework. W. R. Farmer in a recent article rightly showed that the use of palm branches referred to the Maccabees' resistance movement, the remembrance of which certainly played an important role for the Zealots.[11]

The keenest hopes of all Zealotism seemed at last to be on the way toward realisation in Jesus. The entry into Jerusalem surely precipitated Jesus' arrest. Here his enemies had it within their grasp to denounce him to the Romans as a Zealot. The entry could only serve to strengthen the overheated messianic enthusiasm in which the disciples found themselves from there on. We must understand all subsequent events in this light. The words Jesus spoke at the Last Supper must have been a great disillusionment to all his disciples, who even at that time had not yet grasped the sense in which Jesus understood

---

[11] See W. R. Farmer, "The Palm Branches in John 12:13," *Journal of Theological Studies*, 1952, pp. 62ff.

his Messiahship. For a long time he had had to direct their attention to the Suffering Servant of God, whose role he had to fulfill. Sufficient attention has not been given to the fact that the Words of Institution were primarily intended to inform the disciples in clear, unequivocal terms, that Jesus would fulfill his Messiahship as God's Suffering Servant, not as a triumphant Messiah-king of Jerusalem. The two principal motifs of the Suffering Servant songs in Deutero-Isaiah, vicarious suffering and the inauguration of the New Covenant, are also the principal motifs of the Words of Institution.[12] It is not surprising that the Evangelists have linked Judas' betrayal with this last meal. There is at any rate a material connection between this decisive explanation by Jesus of his messianic interpretation and the disillusionment which must account for the basis of Judas' betrayal.[13]

This disillusionment surely seized all the disciples, even if they did not allow themselves to be carried as far as Judas' betrayal. In Gethsemane, in the place where Jesus spent the evening of these last days (this is the fact Judas betrayed), the matter finally came to a head. Here it became conclusively clear that the way of Jesus was radically different from that of the Zealots. But his followers wore swords. They asked whether they should not strike with the sword, and one of them acted on the intention. For Jesus himself, however, Gethsemane was the

[12] See my *Christology of the New Testament,* which is to appear soon.
[13] For the history of the interpretation of the role of Judas Iscariot see K. Lüthi, *Judas Iskariot in der Geschichte der Auslegung,* 1955.

decisive temptation. When he prayed, "If it be possible,
let this cup pass from me," we see wherein the temptation
consisted for him. Rightly Luke connects Gethsemane
with the first temptation. At the end of the temptation
narrative (Luke 4:13) he writes: "The devil left him until another opportunity." Since Luke does not report the
scene with Peter in Caesarea Philippi, only Gethsemane
can mean for him this "other opportunity." Thus in Gethsemane we have to do with the same temptation by the
devil to construe his role as Messiah in political terms. His
disciples—some of them, at least—are armed. Jesus has
many followers in Jerusalem: the entry proved it. And
above all: he is convinced he could pray his Father to
send him "more than twelve legions of angels" (Matt.
26:53). It is the same satanic temptation which, according to Mark, met him at Caesarea Philippi in the person
of Peter. Only here in Gethsemane everything is dramat-
ically heightened. For the soldiers who will arrest him as
a Zealot are on the way, and besides the enticing role of
the Messiah-king there is the purely human dread which
Jesus feels in the face of death. For Jesus is not a Greek
philosopher. Death for him as for Paul is "the last enemy."
Only thus do we grasp the full significance of Jesus' temptation in Gethsemane. And in spite of all, Jesus withstands
even this final temptation to implement the Zealot ideal.
"Put your sword in its sheath!" (Matt. 26:52).

"And then they all forsook him, and fled," writes Mark
(14:50). Jesus was not the one they had so eagerly hoped
for. They had not understood that he had no intention of

being a Zealot leader, an earthly Messiah-king, that on the contrary he regarded this very ideal as inspired by the devil.

Thus it is no wonder that the Roman State also failed to understand the distinctive form of Jesus' claim of divine mission and condemned him to death as an actual Zealot leader, a pretender to the royal throne. For it was by the Roman State, not by the Jews, that Jesus was condemned to death. We cannot treat here in its full breadth this question already raised by Th. Mommsen and J. Juster. In 1931 and after, a lengthy literary controversy on this subject took place in the *Zeitschrift fuer Neutestamentliche Wissenschaft,* a controversy associated with the name of Prof. Hans Lietzmann, the German church historian.[14] According to him the synoptics' whole presentation of an examination before the Jewish Sanhedrin and a condemnation of Jesus by the Sanhedrin is unhistorical. Jesus is not condemned by the Jewish Sanhedrin but by the Romans. The synoptic presentation of the case—implying that Jesus was condemned by the Sanhedrin and that Pilate had only to ratify this judgment—is not true. To prove the thesis just outlined, Lietzmann tries to show

[14] The first impulse was given by the article of H. Lietzmann, *Der Prozess Jesu, Sitzungsbericht der preussischen Akademie der Wissenschaften,* 1931, pp. 313ff. Participants in the further discussion were: M. Dibelius, *Das historische Problem der Leidensgeschichte,* ZNW, 1931, pp. 193ff; H. Lietzmann, *Bemerkungen zum Prozess Jesu,* ZNW, 1931, p. 211ff; Fr. Büchsel, *Die Blutgerichtsbarkeit des Synedrions,* ZNW, 1931, pp. 202ff; H. Lietzmann, *Bemerkungen zum Prozess Jesu II,* ZNW, 1932, pp. 78ff; M. Goguel, *A propos du procès de Jésus,* ZNW, 1934, pp. 84ff. More recently, J. Jeremias, *Zur Geschichtlichkeit des Verhörs vor dem Hohen Rat,* ZNW, 1952, pp. 145ff.

that at that time it was entirely unnecessary for the Jews
to secure Roman ratification of a capital sentence. Thus,
as often happens, the whole controversy got off on a side-
track. The discussion centered exclusively on the juridical
question of the right of the Jews to carry out capital punishment on their own authority. The discussion of this
specialised question yielded no result, and in all probability the question is insoluble. But the principal question—whether Jesus was condemned by the Romans or by
the Jews—was thus lost to view. Yet its answer does not
depend on this side-issue. Even if the Jews were obliged
to have their death-sentences ratified by the Romans, it is
none the less possible that in the case of Jesus no death
sentence was passed by the Jews, but rather that his judicial condemnation was by the Romans. To this extent I
acknowledge the justice of Lietzmann's position. On the
other hand, I do not consider the Jews' examination of
Jesus to be a pure invention. I believe merely that it had,
not the character of a trial, with the passing of a sentence;
but rather that of a hearing aimed at furnishing the basis
for a denunciation of Jesus by the Jewish authorities to
the Romans.

The most important proof that the death sentence was
passed by the Romans and not by the Jews is the form of
capital punishment: crucifixion. That is not a Jewish but
a Roman punishment. If Jesus had been convicted of
blasphemy by the Jews, and if Pilate had merely to ratify
this verdict, Jesus would have been stoned to death.

The inscription over the cross is further confirmation

that Jesus was not condemned by the Jews for blasphemy, but by the Romans as a Zealot, a pretender to the royal throne of Israel. This inscription was not just Pilate's fancy. What we have here is standard procedure, obligatory among the Romans in the case of the passing of a death sentence: the grounds of the verdict had to be posted on the cross. This inscription was defined by a terminus technicus as the "titulus"—a word which the Johannine Gospel has preserved in its Latin form (John 19:19). This titulus states a purely political crime: King of the Jews.

Paradoxical as it may seem after what we have ascertained about Jesus' attitude toward the Zealots, it was as a Zealot leader that he was executed by the Romans. The *legal* responsibility lies at the door of the Romans, not the Jews. The *moral* responsibility, in contrast, lies on the Jewish side. Nevertheless it was not the whole of the Jewish people—this must be emphasised [15]—but a particular class which had an interest in his condemnation and therefore denounced Jesus to the Romans as a Zealot. They may well have known better, since in order to interest Pilate in Jesus' case they changed the meaning of the theological concept of the "Kingdom of God" into a political one. The priestly party of the Sadducees, who collaborated with the Romans, probably played a leading role in the denunciation. It was they who were especially offended by Jesus' cleansing of the temple. But the Phari-

[15] In this respect one must agree with the spiritedly defended thesis of Jules Isaac, *Jésus et Israïl*, 1948.

sees made common cause with the Sadducees: on quite
different grounds, to be sure—grounds of a theological nature. For Jesus had embarrassed them by his preaching,
aimed directly against them and popular with the people.
In respect to their own hostile attitude toward the Romans they could not, of course, stand in the foreground
when it came to denouncing Jesus to the Romans as a
treacherous Zealot. It is much more likely that they
worked against him in secret.

The division of the actual responsibility shared by the
Jewish authorities and the Roman State in Jesus' condemnation is much more correctly reported in the Johannine
Gospel than in the synoptics. I agree at this point in the
main with Maurice Goguel who, as is well known, regards
the Johannine Gospel in many respects as the better
source for the passion narrative.[16] According to the Johannine Gospel the role of the Jewish authorities is confined
to a denunciation of Jesus to the Romans. The trial and
conviction are legally the affair of the Romans only. It
is in itself more than likely that the hearing before the
high priest was not a regular session of the Sanhedrin. It
has been justly pointed out that a night session was contrary to the existing legal stipulations. The hearing did
not have the character of a judicial act, but served to
furnish the testimony necessary to a better foundation
for the denunciation to the Romans. The hearing before

---

[16] More exactly, he assumes that better sources and traditions were avail-
able to the Fourth Evangelist at different points. See M. Goguel,
Jésus, 2nd ed., 1950, pp. 363ff.

the high priest ends thus in Luke also, who so often approximates the Johannine Gospel, not with a judicial sentence, as in Mark and Matthew.

But everything becomes much more clear in the Johannine Gospel. Here Jesus' arrest in Gethsemane is made already by the Roman cohort [17] under the command of the Captain [18] (ch. 18:3). From the beginning the entire action proceeds from the Romans. From the legal standpoint this presupposes that Jesus had been denounced to the Romans even before this time. As a matter of fact we hear this also in another place in the Johannine Gospel. In chapter 11:48ff it is recorded that a decision was made in a session of the Sanhedrin to make sure that the Romans would not hold the whole Jewish people responsible for the unrest which Jesus evoked by his agitation. We read here that Jesus had a great following among the people. The members of the Sanhedrin are afraid they will be suspected of sympathising with this demagogue Jesus. For this reason they seize the initiative. It is not that they themselves are condemning Jesus, for political grounds could not serve as the basis for a Jewish condemnation. The Jewish authorities had not the least intention of assuming responsibility for Jesus' death. For they feared the people, and knew Jesus was popular among them.

What opinion, then, are we to form about the proceedings before the high priest? They did not have the char-

[17] σπεῖρα.   [18] χιλίαρχος.

acter of a trial, but of an unofficial investigation by the
authorities, from which ensued the accusation before the
Romans. Evidently the Romans, who were conscious of
Jesus' popularity, wished to be assured that the highest
Jewish authorities really wanted Jesus condemned. Pilate
wanted to be protected on this flank before he passed
judgment on Jesus. If it is a question, not of a regular trial
before the high priest, but of a mere interrogation, then
we can retain most of what the synoptics record about it,
even though they misunderstood the purpose of the hearing. Once again the Johannine Gospel has quite probably
preserved the better tradition, when it records the real
hearing as having taken place before the past high priest
Annas, and not before the incumbent high priest Caia-
phas as in the synoptics. We know the past high priest
still exercised a high moral authority. Such moral counsel
was important to the Romans. If the affair was in the
hands of the past high priest, then the unofficial character
of the Jewish proceedings becomes still clearer; and the
examination by night, which on the evidence of the Mish-
nah is hardly admissible as a regular session of the Sanhedrin, offers no further difficulties.

Then even the proceedings before Pilate become
much clearer. It has been the custom, as we know, to explain Pilate's hesitation as a fiction attributable to later
apologetic tendencies; and these have certainly influenced
the presentation, especially in the Matthean Gospel. But
the fact that Pilate hesitated and pronounced the death
sentence only with genuine reluctance may be historical.

Not as if Pilate had felt pity, or had even been convinced of Jesus' mission. But he may well have observed (since we have no reason to doubt his intelligence) that the man whom they had haled before him as a political rebel was in reality politically innocuous. He may have regarded him as deluded, and he probably guessed that he had to deal with an intra-Jewish wrangle. But as a representative of the Roman State he dared not discourage those Jews, on whose cooperation he supported his policy in Judaea, when they informed on a Jew as a Zealot leader. Pilate's bearing becomes much clearer when we consider that he had to investigate only the charge of Zealot agitation against the Roman State.

The Barabbas scene also is less impossible, as others have said,[19] when we consider that Pilate and not the Jews passed judgment, and that the denunciation proceeded only from the Jewish upper class and not from the whole people. Pilate must have been concerned not to provoke any ill-humor among the people by his condemnation. Most important for our question about the person of Barabbas, however, is the designation of the crime laid to his charge in Mark 15:7: "He was with the imprisoned rebels who had committed murder *in the insurrection.*" Here no doubt is possible: we have to do with a Zealot uprising, and Barabbas was a Zealot. When he is set alongside Jesus it is quite clear that for the Romans

[19] M. Goguel, *Jésus*, 1950, pp. 382ff., believes the whole scene to be unhistorical. It is true that there are difficulties from the legal point of view, but they are not insurmountable. On this question see J. Merkel, *Die Begnadigung am Passahfeste*, ZNW, 1905, pp. 293ff.

both cases involved the same crime and the same verdict. Jesus like Barabbas was condemned by the Romans and not by the Jews, and in fact *as a Zealot*.

And this explains also one of Jesus' last sayings, which is almost never explained aright, because the whole situation which we have found here is not taken into account. On the way to the place of execution Jesus says to the weeping women (in Luke 23:28–30); "Daughters of Jerusalem, do not weep for me, but weep for yourselves and for your children . . . For if they do this to the green wood, what shall be done to the dry?" All exegetes agree that Jesus refers to himself as the green wood. But who are the subject of "they do"? And why does Jesus refer to himself as the green wood? I believe there can be no doubt in this situation, where Jesus is being led to the place of execution by the Romans, that only the Romans can be the subject of the sentence. Then the saying of Jesus can have only the following meaning: If the Romans execute *me* as a Zealot, who am no Zealot and who have always warned against Zealotism, what will they do then to the true Zealots! For the Romans Jesus was in reality green wood, for he had indeed renounced Zealotism. Then this saying of Jesus expresses exactly what I have endeavored to show here: 1) Throughout his entire ministry Jesus had to come to terms with Zealotism; 2) He renounced Zealotism, although he also assumed a critical attitude toward the Roman State; 3) He was condemned to death as a Zealot by the Romans.

I have mentioned Robert Eisler's thesis which, by a

wresting of the text, makes Jesus a Zealot. This thesis has been justly rejected. Jesus was no Zealot. But the historians have thrown out the baby with the bath. They have not paid attention to the fact that Jesus' whole ministry was in continuous contact with Zealotism, that this formed the background, so to speak, of his activity, and that he was executed as a Zealot. I believe also that the Slavic translation of the Jewish historiographer Josephus, which admittedly presents Jesus' movement as Zealotist,[20] could have at least a kernel of reality underlying it. The misuse which Eisler and his disciples have practised on these texts is probably to be blamed also, in part at least, for the fact that many have eliminated them all too quickly as completely worthless historically.[21]

Jesus' saying about the green wood and the dry, his expression about what is to be returned to Caesar and what to God, and finally the titulus over the cross: "King of the Jews," furnish the best description of what we have established in both these chapters about Jesus' attitude toward the State.

Before we speak about "Paul and the State" in our next chapter we shall take a moment to indicate the theological consequences of our findings to this point.

[20] A. Berendts, *Die Zeugnisse vom Christentum im slavischen "de bello Judaico" des Josephus,* 1906; A. Berendts and K. Grass, *Flavius Josephus vom jüdischen Kriege nach der slavischen Ubersetzung deutsch herausgegeben und mit dem griechischen Text verglichen,* 1924/27.

[21] Also M. Goguel contests their genuineness in various publications. See his *Jésus,* 1950, pp. 63ff.

III.

Paul and the State

Is THERE a direct line from Jesus' attitude toward the State to that of the Apostle Paul? In order to be able to decide, we ask first of all: What consequences for the problem, "Gospel and State," follow from Jesus' teaching and life as we have presented them in the previous chapters?

1. Jesus does not regard the State as a final institution to be equated somehow with the Kingdom of God. The State belongs to the age which still exists even now, but which will definitely vanish as soon as the Kingdom of God comes. Accordingly Jesus' disciples have both the right and the duty to judge the State on the basis of their knowledge of the coming Kingdom and of the will of

God. As long as this age still continues, however, the *existence* of the State is willed by God—even the existence of the heathen Roman State, although it is not of divine nature. Consequently it is not the business of the disciple of Jesus to assume the initiative in abolishing this State as an institution. Rather he is to give the State what it needs for its existence. On the other hand, as soon as the State demands more than is necessary to its existence, as soon as it demands what is God's—thus transgressing its limits—the disciple of Jesus is relieved of all obligation to *this* requirement of a totalitarian State. According to Jesus' command, he is not allowed to give to a State what is God's. But he will not deny even to a totalitarian State those things, like taxes, which are necessary to the existence of any State. We shall see that there was indeed one point at which the Roman State was totalitarian: namely, emperor worship. At this point the disciple of Jesus has to proclaim that the State has transgressed its limits and has demanded what belongs to God; and he himself will not give to the State this which is unjustly required of him. But he will nevertheless pay taxes to it; and he will not take it upon himself in the name of the Gospel to proceed against the State by force of arms.

Jesus does not furnish an exact definition of what is Caesar's and what is God's. Consequently there can be border cases which can be decided only on the basis of the whole Gospel. Still, a pointer can be found in the fact that in Mark 12 it is money that is to be given to Caesar.

2. Jesus agrees with Zealotism insofar as it takes se-

riously the expectation of the Kingdom of God and thus does not regard the existing Roman State as an ultimate, divine institution. On the other hand he radically divorces himself from the Zealots insofar as they intend to establish the Kingdom of God on their own by human strength, insofar as they do not acknowledge that this age, with the institution of the State, is willed by God. They have a false expectation of the Kingdom of God. Therefore they want to initiate a holy war and to establish within a human framework a Kingdom of God which is an earthly kingdom and which at the same time takes the place of the Roman Empire. Jesus sees that use of this method places one on exactly the same plane as every other totalitarian State. This is also an abandonment of the New Testament expectation of a kingdom which is really God's, and not a human kingdom. If the Zealots succeed in realising their ideal, it will be a totalitarian State of the most extreme form; one making divine claims. Their whole struggle against the Roman Empire is therefore meaningless, since it also leads to a totalitarian State: the theocratic State. We see it is from exactly *the same* eschatological attitude that Jesus condemns at one and the same time every absolutising of the Roman State *and* the waging of war against this State. Jesus' attitude only *seems* to be contradictory. In reality it is thoroughly logical, since it has its basis in one and the same expectation of the End. To the Roman State the disciple of Jesus must say: Give God what is his; therefore do not give it to the State. To the Zealots Jesus has to say: Give the

Roman Caesar what is his; therefore do not make a political State out of the community which is to proclaim the Kingdom of God.

Does this thereby condemn all resistance against a State which transgresses its limits? No, we have seen that where this State demands what belongs to God the disciple of Jesus has to make this illegitimate trespass known on the basis of the Gospel of Jesus, and he *dare not* give the State what is God's; he dare not, for example, advocate a doctrine which sets idols in God's place. But even in this case the community of the disciples of Jesus does not have to launch a *holy war*. Waging war may be a matter for the State, but not for the community of the disciples.

3. We ask finally: In the case of Jesus' condemnation did the Roman State transgress its limits as a State? If the accusation that Jesus was a Zealot had corresponded with the facts, then the State would have remained within the limits of its rights. If Jesus had really been a Zealot, then it would not have been a totalitarian excess, but rather a legitimate procedure undertaken by the State against one of its enemies. (This is not meant to imply that capital punishment is regarded as legitimate in principle: this question is not under discussion here.) I only wish to emphasise that a distinction exists between the later Christian martyrs, who were executed for refusing to meet a totalitarian demand of the State—namely the worship of Caesar—and the condemnation of Jesus which came only as the result of a question of order, of the se-

curity of the State. For the later Christian martyrs it is
the totalitarian State which demands what belongs to
God. This is not the case in the condemnation of Jesus.
The injustice of the Roman State in condemning Jesus
does not consist in a totalitarian excess, but in the fact
that it did not take the trouble to ascertain and to *understand* Jesus' *real* attitude—not even to the extent of understanding as much about it as a non-Christian State is
able to understand. Namely, that Jesus was in no sense
an enemy of the State on principle, but rather a loyal
citizen who offered no threat to the State's existence.
Granted that on the basis of his consciousness of mission
and his expectation of the Kingdom of God he did not
regard the State as a final, divine institution, even where
it observed its proper limits. He regarded it as a temporary institution, toward which he maintained a critical
attitude. He refused obedience only to the totalitarian
State which was exceeding its limits, drawing the line
always at the point where the State demanded what is
God's—but only at that point.

In subsequent generations even until today, defective
understanding of the true Christian attitude toward the
State, and above all, false interpretation of the Christian
expectation of the End have provoked States to persecution. The Christians' expectation of the End has been even
further misconstrued, as if Christians were enemies of
the State on principle, anarchists. In reality the Christians'
expectation of the End is the hope for a kingdom which
comes only from God, not one which men undertake to

establish on their own by the destruction of the framework of this present age to which the institution of the State belongs. The consequence of this expectation, therefore, is that this framework is accepted as willed by God, and that *within* this framework the disciple of Jesus works for the coming Kingdom, thus remaining loyal to the State even though, to be sure, he is in principle critical.

Many a persecution of Christians could have been avoided if the State had taken the pains to *understand* their attitude and to convince itself of their loyalty. The cross of Christ in itself should remind all responsible statesmen to examine the Christians' real attitude toward the State.[1]

It is all the more important to gain precise knowledge of the New Testament attitude toward the State. This is especially true of the Apostle Paul's interpretation of the State. Here things have come to such a pass that men are willing to classify Paul as an almost servile, uncritical servant of any State, as if he would say Yea and Amen to every claim of the State, be it never so totalitarian. They base their case on the single Pauline statement in the Epistle to the Romans, 13:1: "Let every man be subject to the powers prevailing over us." Few sayings in the New Testament have suffered as much misuse as this

[1] John Knox, "Pliny and I Peter: A Note on I Peter 4:14–16 and 3:15," *Journal of Biblical Literature*, 1955, pp. 187ff, rightly shows that for these same reasons the Christians in I Peter are reminded that it is also their duty to instruct the State concerning the true attitude of Christians.

one. As soon as Christians, out of loyalty to the Gospel of
Jesus, offer resistance to a State's totalitarian claim, the
representatives of that State, or their collaborationist
theological advisers, are accustomed to appeal to this saying of Paul, as if Christians are here commanded to en-
dorse and thus to abet all the crimes of a totalitarian State.

If this were really Paul's opinion, it would stand in
flagrant contradiction to that of Jesus. But it would also
contradict the opinion of other New Testament authors
as well, chiefly that of the author of the Johannine Apocalypse. Above all, moreover, Paul would contradict himself.
For we find in Paul exactly the same thing we find in
Jesus: side by side stand two sorts of assertions, which
seem to be contradictory, but actually proceed from one
and the same fundamental attitude. Thus we find in the
Pauline epistles not only this most famous passage, Romans 13:1ff, but also quite different passages, chiefly I
Cor. 6:1ff and I Cor. 2:8. With Paul also, just as with
Jesus, both classes of texts must be borne in mind and
considered together. The fountainhead of all false biblical
interpretation and of all heresy is invariably the isolation
and the absolutising of one single passage. This applies
most especially to the interpretation of Romans 13:1ff.

But it is necessary not only to confront this passage
with the other Pauline passages which contain, directly or
indirectly, Paul's opinion of the State: it is also necessary
above all to consider the context of the passage at hand.
Even this connection is all too often disregarded. But this
context teaches us two things: First, the matter under

discussion at this point is the Christian commandment of love—evil is not to be rewarded with evil, rather one is to do good to his enemy. This stands in Romans 12 immediately before the section about the State in Romans 13:1ff; and directly afterwards, in verse 8, the same theme is resumed. Second, the expectation of the End is also under discussion: the night is far spent, the day draws near (Rom. 13:11ff).

This background to the section is important, and shows in itself that there can be no question here of an unconditional and uncritical subjection to any and every demand of the State. It arises immediately out of the context that the State does properly exactly the opposite of what the Christian is to do: it takes vengeance on him who does evil (verse 4). Immediately before this (ch. 12:17) it is stated that the Christian on the contrary is by no means to repay evil with evil. *Nevertheless* we are to accept the State; thus in spite of the fact that it does exactly the opposite of what the Christian is to do, we are to submit ourselves to the State as such. For if it takes vengeance, it does so as "the servant of God"; v. 4: "It is God's servant for vengeance upon the evil-doer." Even if it does not know this itself, it stands nevertheless unconsciously in the service of God. How this is possible, is not explicitly explained. We shall ask at the end of this work if there is not an implicit answer to this question.

Therefore we are not to oppose the State because it represents other than Christian principles. The State is concerned with the judicial principle of the retribution of evil. Indeed it even bears the sword, we hear in v. 4, while the Christian is not to kill. Only God may take vengeance, and he avails himself of the service of the State for this purpose. For even the heathen State, insofar as it really is a state, knows how to distinguish between good and evil. This is explicitly stated in this section: vv. 3, 4. Only he who does evil has to fear the State (which really is a State); not he who does good. The State, therefore, has sound judgment over good and evil. Only its bearing toward evil is not the same as that which is appropriate to the Christian; and yet the Christian is to subordinate himself to the State in its proper sphere. Therefore a "nevertheless" is to be fixed above this command of Paul. Paul does not consider it self-evident in and of itself that the Christian is to recognise the existence of the State. Just for this reason it is necessary for him to give an explicit commandment about this to the Romans to whom he is writing here. It is not self-evident, for the State proceeds according to the principle, not of love, but of retribution.

We dare not forget that the readers found themselves in the very capital of the Roman Empire, and that precisely among the Christians there it was possible for a temper of animosity toward the State to arise similar to that of the Jewish Zealots. This renders more understandable Paul's command.

The context in which this section about the State stands and in which Christian love is discussed, shows plainly that here just as in the teaching of Jesus the only

thing repudiated is the renunciation of the validity of
the State as a matter of principle. Basically, the paragraph
states no more and no less than the saying of Jesus:
"Render unto Caesar the things that are Caesar's; and to
God the things that are God's." It is probable that the
Apostle even alludes to this saying in v. 7, when he speaks
of the tribute which is to be given to whom it is due.
"Pay all of them, what is due them," he writes at the
beginning of the verse. In the background, then, the tacit
negative amplification stands here as well: "Do not give
them what is not their due." Let us not forget that it is
Nero's State which is under discussion here—the same
State which will demand of the Christians things which
do not belong to it. Paul does not speak of these things
here. His own condemnation however proves that he does
not recommend subjection in these things. But where it
is a question of the existence of the State, the commandment stands none the less: "Give even to this State its
due." For the fact that there still is a State is willed by
God. The present age still endures.

And this brings us to the second of the declarations
mentioned previously as important in connection with
our paragraph: the expectation of the End, about which
Paul speaks in equally close connection, in v. 11. This
connection reminds us that the State is a temporary institution. As for Jesus, this has two implications: 1. The
State is nothing final, nothing absolute. It will pass away.
2. For the duration of this present age it is not, indeed, a
divine entity, but it is nevertheless willed by God as a

temporary institution. God makes use of the State as long
as this age endures, and therefore *we* as Christians do
not have to oppose the institution of the State as such, but
rather have to acknowledge its existence.

That is the meaning of the admonitions in Romans
13:1ff as they arise from the context.

And now let us confront this passage with the other:
I Cor. 6:1ff. Whoever interprets Romans 13:1ff without
reference to its context, must necessarily find a complete
contradiction between Romans 13:1ff and I Cor. 6:1ff.
But today [2] this passage is usually entirely overlooked when
Paul's opinion of the State is under discussion. And yet
this is the problem dealt with in this passage too, and
indeed it touches upon a specially important institution
of the State: the administration of justice, which is mentioned precisely in Romans 13:1ff. Here in I Cor. 6 Paul
orders the Corinthian Christians not to bring their controversies before the State's courts of justice. If they already have lawsuits among themselves, which is sad
enough, they ought at least to settle them among themselves, within the congregation, and not before heathen
judges. In Romans 13:1ff Paul says precisely about the
heathen State that it knows how to judge, that it knows
how to discriminate between good and evil and that it
punishes only the evil. And now we read here, on the
contrary: the Christians are to keep away from this insti-

[2] In contrast to the older exegetes who, all too often, through a misunderstanding of Rom. 13:1ff saw 1 Cor. 6:1ff in a false light. See
L. Vischer's thorough work, *Die Auslegungsgeschichte von 1 Kor.
6:1–11*, 1955.

tution! Is there really a contradiction here? Even here
Paul does not in any sense deny the State the right to
administer its own judicial affairs. Neither does he say
that this administration of justice is bad or in opposition
to God. What is said in Romans 13:1ff may be valid here
as well. It stands in the background of I Cor. 6, but is
not explicit here, just as what is said in I Cor. 6 stands in
the background of the Romans passage, but is not explicit
there.

For the settlement of their quarrels Christians are not
to make use of the State's legitimate institution of justice.
Here we see clearly that for Paul there exists a limit to
the recognition of any State. Even to the extent that it
remains within its legitimate limits (and the administration of justice in the Roman State is a legitimate function)
the State is nothing absolute, nothing final.[3] Everywhere
the Christian can dispense with the State without threat-
ening its existence, he should do so. The existence of the
State will not be threatened if the Christians avoid bringing their litigation before the State and use ecclesiastical
justice in their congregations. This does not mean that
they will also take over the other affairs of the State. But
admittedly this chapter shows us in an especially clear
manner that it is false to ascribe to Paul in Romans 13:1ff

[3] J. Héring, *A Good and a Bad Government According to the New Testa-*
ment, 1954, pp. 47ff, does not speak of this "limitation" of the recognition due even to the legitimate State. He speaks only of the limits
set for our obedience to the totalitarian State. Since this short writing
of Héring is more of a popular nature, the problems in it are necessarily somewhat simplified. Concerning the rejection of my interpretation of the ἐξουσίαι in Romans 13:1 (pp. 13ff), see the Excursus, p. 93.

the opinion that the State is by nature a divine form and that its principles are equally valid as those Jesus deduced from the expectation of the Kingdom of God.

It is false to read Romans 13:1ff apart from I Cor. 6:1ff, and it is false to read I Cor. 6:1ff apart from Rom. 13:1ff. The State is not simply divine, as is usually inferred from Romans 13:1ff. It is merely *willed* by God, "*ordained* of God." It is not unintentional that there is in the first verse what amounts to a piling up of Greek words containing the Greek root "order." [4] It corresponds to God's order that there is a State *even now*, as long as this age endures. For the duration of this age the State is *willed* of God, but it is not divine in *nature*. If it were of divine nature, then according to Paul the Christians could bring their litigation before the State just as well as before the congregation. Here we see the limit which is set to all affirmation, even of the legitimate State: it is a temporary institution. Neither is it unintentional that the admonition in I Cor. 6:1ff finds its rationale in the *expectation of the End:* the Christians are not to bring their quarrels into the national courts of justice, because they themselves, indeed, have been called to judge angels at the last day. We shall see that it is of special significance that the Christians' final judgment upon the *angels* is mentioned in just this connection.

First, however, a third Pauline text remains to be named: I Cor. 2:8: "None of the rulers of this world understood the wisdom of God; for if they had understood

---

4 τάξις.

it they would not have crucified the Lord of glory." The
Greek expression for "rulers of this world," [5] to the profane reader means merely "earthly political rulers." But
to Jewish readers it has still another meaning: namely,
"demonic, invisible powers which stand behind all earthly
happenings and use human beings as their effective
agents." When Paul the Jew uses this expression it is certain that in using this designation current in the Judaism
of his time he is thinking also of these invisible forces and
powers—all the more certain, since they play so great a
role in his own thinking and above all in the thinking of
the first Christians. But it is equally certain that at the
same time he is speaking of the effective agents: namely,
the earthly rulers, the Roman administrators of Palestine.
This follows clearly from the parallels in Acts 3:17 and
13:27f; and especially from the fact that mention is made
of the crucifixion of Jesus, which took place in the thoroughly empirical framework of history. The question is
not posed here in the form of alternatives: whether Paul
has in mind here only the invisible, demonic powers or
whether he has in mind here only Pilate and Herod. He
speaks of both.[6] But then it is important that here he sees
the worldly rulers as the effective tools of the invisible
powers. This too belongs to the idea Paul has of the State.

It is to be observed further that the Apostle mentions
here the motif of ignorance, of failure to recognise: the
rulers of the world did not know whom they were crucify-

---

[5] ἄρχοντες τοῦ αἰῶνος τούτου.

[6] For details on this question, see Excursus, p. 93.

ing! Paul means this in the theological sense. But we remember also what we have said about Jesus' condemnation by the Romans: the inscription on the cross, which
brands Jesus with the crime of being a Zealot, proves that
one of history's greatest miscarriages of justice transpired
there. For Paul, however, this error born of ignorance
assumes cosmic dimensions: the invisible powers which
stood behind Pilate had no inkling that this crucifixion
spelled their own defeat. For this reason Pilate finds his
way into the Creed.

Romans 13:1ff, I Cor. 6:1ff, and I Cor. 2:8, taken together, furnish a uniform picture, which coincides as-
tonishingly with Jesus' conception of the State. I have
shown in various publications that in II Thess. 2:6 the
State *cannot* be the subject of discussion, as many have
long believed.[7] Hence we cite only the three Pauline
texts already named.

What consequences can we draw from them for the
problem "Paul and the State"? The State in itself is nothing divine. But it maintains a certain dignity in that it
stands in an order which is *still* willed by God. Hence it
is true for Paul also: the Christian is commanded on the
basis of the Gospel to maintain a critical attitude toward

---

[7] *Christ and Time,* p. 145. Even if my own explanation of this passage
should not be valid, in any case the reference of the κατέχων to the
State must be considered the least probable hypothesis. The whole
late Jewish and early Christian apocalyptic (also II Thess. 2:4 in the
same section we are considering!) thought of the Empire as a satanic
embodiment. It would therefore be a remarkable confusion of thought
if II Thess. 2:6 ascribed to the Empire the role of him whose task is
to arrest the work of Anti-Christ.

the State; but he has to give the State all that is necessary to its existence. He has to affirm the State as an institution. Of the totalitarian claim of the State which demands for itself what is God's, Paul does not speak directly. But there can be no doubt that he too would not
have allowed the Christians to obey the State just at
the point where it demands what is God's. What we know
about his *life*, proves this. He would not have permitted
them to say "Caesar is Lord" and "anathema Jesus" (let
Jesus be accursed), as this was demanded by the same
Roman State to which the Christian is to pay taxes and
whose institution he is to acknowledge as willed by God.

This attitude of Paul achieves a new theological depth,
however, and is placed in the context of his whole theology when we consider one final point. In all three Pauline texts which speak of the State there is direct or indirect reference to the angelic powers which stand behind the State. This is particularly clear in I Cor. 2:8,
where "the rulers of this world" are mentioned. But we
have seen that in I Cor. 6 as well Paul offers as his reason
for the command to shun the national courts of justice the
fact that the Christians will one day judge the "angels."
In late Judaism "angels" imply both good and bad angels.
On the whole, they are invisible powers which are at work
behind every visible happening. The Christians are not
to allow their controversies to be judged by the State,
because the Christians themselves will one day sit in
judgment over the powers which now stand invisible behind the State. Further, even in the famous passage in

Romans 13:1ff Paul uses a Greek expression (*exousiai*)
which, exactly like the designation, "rulers of this world,"
refers in profane Greek indeed to the earthly authorities,
the State, but at the same time means to Jewish readers
"invisible powers." Paul does not write: "Let every man
be subject to the State!" He does mean the State, to be
sure. But he writes: "Let every man be subject to the
powers that be!" The Greek word for powers which
stands here, exousiai, Paul uses in *every* other passage
(and he speaks of them often) to refer to invisible angelic
powers and forces. There is not a single other Pauline
passage where Paul means anything else than angelic
powers by this word in its plural form. The paragraph,
Romans 13:1ff, obviously speaks of the State. And it is
self-evident that Paul also knows that the word means
"State" in profane Greek, just as he knows in I Cor. 2:8
that the word used there means "earthly rulers." But it is
then quite likely that in Romans 13:1ff as well Paul has
in mind that the State which we are to affirm as an institution is the effective agent of those invisible powers. The
word "powers," then, exactly like the word "rulers" in I
Cor. 2:8 has a double meaning. It means here at once
"angelic powers" and "State."

I have intentionally reserved this point until the close
of the discussion. For the New Testament scholars in
Germany are accustomed to reject the connection between Romans 13:1ff and the angelic powers. In reply to
their objections I have recently made my case for the
probability of this relationship in detail in an article

which is added as an "Excursus" to the present work.[8]
But I have shown in this chapter that even *quite apart
from this connection between the State and the angelic
powers* Paul's attitude toward the State is quite clear,
when we consider Romans 13:1ff and I Cor. 6:1ff together.
It finds, however, confirmation and depth when we bear
this connection with the powers in mind; and the acceptance of this connection also in Romans 13:1ff is indicated
all the more clearly, since it is obvious in both other passages which speak of the State, I Cor. 6:1ff and 2:8. Then,
indeed, we understand better this "nevertheless" which
according to the context alone stands over the whole section Romans 13:1ff. Then we understand that the State is
fundamentally *not* of *divine* nature; that nevertheless on
the basis of a provisional order things are such that this
State can be *God's servant* and we have to submit ourselves to it. Especially the question how a heathen State
is able to distinguish between good and evil, can, at least
implicitly, be answered in the light of this point.

For the first Christians, and Paul above all, had a quite
precise conception of the role of these powers in the
drama of salvation: namely, of their subjection to Christ.
From the fact that the belief in these invisible powers is
far removed from our modern thinking, we dare not conclude that such a belief was merely an incidental, unim-
portant form of expression for Paul and for the first Christians. We dare not ask too quickly: Can we *accept* this

---

[8] See p. 93. The article appeared first in *Theologische Zeitschrift*, 1954,
pp. 321ff.

belief? First of all we ought to *listen* to what the New
Testament says, and to ask what importance it attributes to certain conceptions. Even in Jesus' time this belief
in invisible powers was very important for the Jews: and
special mention should be made here of the Jewish belief
in national guardian-angels, attested chiefly in the book
of Daniel and the books of Enoch. The contemporary application of one and the same word for demonic *and* for
earthly rulers had already been made in the case of the
Hebrew word "śar."

But of especial importance to us is what Paul and the
whole of primitive Christianity teach about these "powers." In my essay on the oldest creedal formulae I have
shown that in all these early formulae (which are thus
older than the so-called Apostles' Creed), mention is regularly made of the fact that by his death Jesus has conquered these powers.[9] Mention of this in these brief
formulae in which the first Christians gathered together
only the most important points of their faith proves how
significant for them was this belief in the conquest of the
powers.

Now in this victory over the angelic powers the whole
chronological tension is attested which is so characteristic for the New Testament situation: in the formulae
mentioned and in other New Testament texts it is said
that these powers have already been vanquished (Col.
1:16ff; 2:15; Phil. 2:10): [10] in other texts, on the contrary,

---

[9] *The Earliest Christian Confessions*, 1949, pp. 59ff.
[10] Also I Peter 3:22.

the conquest by Christ is still an expectation (I Cor. 15:25;
Heb. 10:13). Both views were maintained by the first
Christians. Did they reflect on a connection of the two
expressions? The author of the Johannine Apocalypse
certainly did. He sees the explanation in the temporary
binding of Satan. So we shall probably have to acknowledge for Paul too that he is convinced the decisive victory over the powers has already been achieved; they
have been brought into subjection and stand in the service of Christ. But, to use a figure of speech, the rope with
which they are bound can be lengthened, so that these
powers are able even now to attempt to emancipate themselves. But then their demonic nature becomes visible.
As long as they remain in bondage to Christ, however,
they stand in God's order. Therefore it is proper to be
subject to them to the extent that they stay within their
limits; for to that extent they are God's servants and have
indeed sound judgment over good and evil. Only when
they try to free themselves from the subjection which has
already been realised, and become "totalitarian," to use
this modern word, only then do they demand what belongs to God. Therefore they must finally be conquered
yet again, at the end of days, although the issue has already been decided.

Against the background of this belief in the vanquished
powers at work behind earthly happenings it becomes
especially clear that the State is now a temporary institution not of divine nature but nevertheless willed by God;
that we must remain critical toward every State; that we

must none the less obey every State as far as it remains within its bounds.

But particularly, from this point of view, we shall understand how in the same New Testament in which we read the words from Romans 13:1: "Let every man be subject," and the rulers are "God's servants"; we hear also about this same State—Nero's State—(in Rev. 13) that it is "the beast from the abyss." Now this is spoken from the point where this State is trying to free itself from its subordination and is becoming satanic in that it is demanding what is God's. The State which makes itself independent, which absolutises itself, deifies itself, is precisely the classic expression of the Anti-Christ; just as in the temptation narrative the power of the Devil appears in the fact that he has—or thinks he has—the disposal of the kingdoms of the world. We shall have to speak of this in our last chapter.

NOTE

We have not devoted a special chapter to the two passages I Peter 2:13f and Titus 3:1f, because, with most exegetes, we recognise a material and perhaps literary relationship between them and Rom. 13:1ff. See especially E. G. Selwyn, *The First Epistle of St. Peter,* 1949, pp. 426ff, who also includes I Timothy 2:1ff (see p. 84) and recognises in all four passages a common source, to which I Peter 2:13f stands closest.

IV. *The State in the Johannine Apocalypse*

In the Johannine Apocalypse the problem of the State is quite clear and unequivocal. The complexity we found with Jesus and Paul does not exist here. This is not because the attitude toward the State is any different here from what it was with Jesus and Paul. The reason for the lack of complexity is rather that the same State of which Paul speaks in such positive terms in Romans 13 is judged here exclusively with reference to that excess which finds its most extreme expression in the Roman worship of the Caesar. We have seen that this excess was not in the perspective of Romans 13:1ff. There only the institution of the State as such was under discussion. Similarly here in the Johannine Apocalypse attention is centered on that other aspect, where the State demands what is God's, where it frees itself from the "order" and becomes a satanic power. If the connection between the State and the subjugated angelic powers lies in the background of the Pauline interpretation, then the relationship of Paul to the Johannine Apocalypse—which exists anyhow—becomes clearer. We can go even farther and say that in the Johannine Apocalypse we find a further and indeed very strong support for the interpretation we have given of the theological background of the Pauline interpretation of the State. We have seen that in all three Pauline texts which speak of the State, an expression is used which refers to the invisible powers that stand behind the State even to the extent that it really is, as in Romans 13, God's servant.

In the Johannine Apocalypse this is quite clear. Here there is no problem in this connection. The beast from the abyss, of which Chapter 13 speaks in such strong language, is the Roman Empire. It can probably stand as universally agreed today that we have to do here not with *mythology alone*. To be sure, here as throughout the Johannine Apocalypse mythological motifs are used. This in E. Lohmeyer's famous interpretation is correct.[1] But one will hardly agree with him when he rejects every reference to temporal events.[2] Rather is it clear that under-

[1] E. Lohmeyer, *Die Offenbarung des Johannes,* 2nd ed., published after the author's death by G. Bornkamm, 1953.
[2] M. Rissi, *Zeit und Geschichte in der Offenbarung des Johannes,* 1952 shows very well that Lohmeyer's thesis of timelessness is untenable. Nevertheless, precisely in his exegesis of chapter 13 he is somewhat too strongly influenced by Lohmeyer, when he rejects the connection with the emperor cult. See pp. 77ff. The concepts empire and emperor

lying the whole of the Johannine Apocalypse is the outlook which sees powerful engagements between invisible
warlike powers taking place behind earthly happenings.
Thus it is almost universally acknowledged that the "beast
from the abyss" in Rev. 13 is the Roman Empire insofar as
it requires the worship of the emperor; therewith at the
same time, moreover, every earthly empire of any age so
far as it assumes the role of a totalitarian power. We are
reminded of the temptation narrative in Matthew 4 and
Luke 4, where too it is Satan who offers Christ power over
the kingdoms of the world. The Roman Empire of his
time served the author as an example by which to describe
every empire insofar as it is demonic.

In Romans 13 Paul says of the powers (*exousiai*) that
they stand within God's order and that we must therefore
obey them. Here they have emancipated themselves; or
rather they believe they have done so (for in reality they
have already been conquered); and have thus become
thoroughly satanic. The beast which rises from the abyss
stands indeed in the service of the dragon, Satan (v. 2).
Satan gives him his power, throne, and great authority.

It is characteristic that governmental power exceeding
its proper bounds is generally regarded as the most tangi-
ble embodiment of satanic power. This did not appear for

cult are in apocalyptic writings already a part of the traditional theological description of the Anti-Christ. The assumption of a "political"
reference would have completely agreed with Rissi's main thesis. K. L.
Schmidt, *Das Gegenüber von Kirche und Staat in der Gemeinde des
Neuen Testaments, Theol. Blätter,* 1937, pp. 1ff, emphatically carries
out this "political" interpretation.

the first time in Christianity; it had already been the case
long since in Judaism. The grandiose description of the
beast which is given in chapter 13 by the author of the
Johannine Apocalypse at the very beginning of the chapter
makes use of the familiar features with which the four
beasts in the seventh chapter of the book of Daniel are
described. Already in the book of Daniel these four beasts
are the four kingdoms of the world. In the Johannine
Apocalypse the features of all earthly kingdoms are brought
together, concentrated in the *one* beast. It bears the features of the cunning panther, the strong bear, and the lion
with yawning jaws. The commentators justly refer to the
Old Testament parallels which have contributed to this
description.[3] One could also write a commentary on this
chapter in which one adduced parallels from history, up
to the very latest moment of our present time. The description is that realistic. It remains a most noteworthy
fact that according to the Jewish, as to the early Christian,
outlook the totalitarian State is precisely the classic form
of the Devil's manifestation on earth.

Thus he is described for us in grandiose style: his
mighty success is mentioned (v. 4): the beast arouses
astonishment, the whole world, it is said, is in his train.
We are reminded of the power of attraction all totalitarian states exercise upon the masses. They fall down

[3] Besides Lohmeyer, see the following newer commentaries among
others: R. H. Charles, *The Revelation of St. John*, Vol. II, 1920; E. B.
Allo, *St. Jean, L'Apocalypse*, 1921; W. Hadorn, *Die Offenbarung des
Johannes*, 1947; C. Brütsch, *Clarté de l'Apocalypse*, 4th ed., 1955.

before the dragon itself, who has given the beast its commission, and before the beast as well.

It belongs to the Devil's inmost nature that he imitates God. This is particularly characteristic for the satanic State described here, the beast which has been unchained and which has freed itself from the divine order. With its totalitarian claim it demands what is God's, but it generally advances this claim by applying to itself all of God's attributes. It is just this religious claim of the State which constitutes the satanic! Looking back from this vantage point to Jesus' renunciation of the messianism of the Zealots, we understand much better the exclamation, "Get thee behind me, Satan!" which he addressed to all who wished to divert him onto this path.

The mimicry of God is displayed in the fact that the worshipping masses acclaim the beast in the very words which, according to Exodus 15:11, are proper to God alone: "Who is like unto thee!" (v. 4). In fact the Devil tries to imitate even the divine suffering (v. 3).

In addition mention is made of his boastful behavior. But his huge mouth is able to utter only blasphemies (v. 6). His specialty consists in waging war. His battle involves the saints. According to chapter 17 he finds allies for this battle among the kings. And he succeeds in conquering the saints in all the world, it is said in chapter 13; and everyone in all the world falls down before him (v. 8). The apostasy of the saints before this national power is great. If, resisting the temptation to illustrate this from the most recent past, we wish to find confirmation for it in Christian antiquity, we need only remember what Pliny says as early as the beginning of the second century about the apostasy of the Christians who were forced to offer sacrifice to Caesar as God. Or we may recall what we hear from the time of Decius of the alarmingly frequent instances of abjuration of the Christian faith.

But allusion is made here also to those who did *not* bow down before the beast. These are they whose names (as is said in v. 8) are written in the book of life.

What we hear about the second beast, which comes out of the earth, is still clearer. In chapters 16:13; 19:20; and 20:10 this second beast is identified with the false prophet. He stands in the service of the first beast, in the service of the totalitarian State. Here the description is so plain and so concrete that we can say flatly: the second beast represents the religio-ideological propaganda authority of the totalitarian State. In this pseudo-religious pretension is displayed the satanic character of this false prophet who presents himself as a true prophet of the true God. In reality he makes propaganda for the one who assigned him his commission, the Devil, the totalitarian State. Precisely at this point the necessity is revealed which obliges the Devil to imitate God, the false prophet to imitate the true. Every totalitarian State needs an ideology which is a parody of faith.

Anyone who has the feeling here that by use of these expressions I have modernised the Apocalypse altogether

too far is invited to read the thirteenth chapter for himself. It is said of the second beast that it deceives the inhabitants of the earth with all sorts of miracles which it
performs in the strength of the first beast (v. 14). He
orders the inhabitants of the earth to set up an image of
the first beast and worship it. Whoever does not worship
this image is slain. There can be no doubt that the reference
here is to the worship of the emperor. We need only hold
alongside it the report made to Trajan by Pliny, the gover-
nor of Bithynia. The Christians who had been arrested
were forced to offer sacrifice before an image of Caesar,
kept at hand for this purpose, and to say *Kyrios Kaisar*
and "Let Christ be accursed." If they did this they were
set free; if not, they were condemned to death.

In our thirteenth chapter of the Apocalypse we hear
further (in v. 17) that those who have worshipped the
image are furnished a receipt. They have an official brand
affixed as a sign that they have submitted to the worship
of the emperor. We know that in the later persecution of
Christians official receipts for sacrifices were provided.
Here it is said—probably it is a figure of speech—that the
mark was branded on their forehead. This calls to mind
the oriental custom according to which the name of a
heathen deity was scratched into the skin of its servants
in order to designate them as the property of this divinity.
It may be that Paul makes reference to this practice in
Galatians 6:17 when he says that *he* bears the marks of
Christ, the Lord to whom he belongs. In the Johannine
Apocalypse it is said, in chapter 7, that the elect are sup-

plied with a divine seal. Here too, therefore, the author
considers that the Devil imitates God in this point as in
all other things as well. However that may be, we have
to do here with a receipt furnished by the State for worship offered to Caesar's image. Those who do not bear
the sign representing the self-deifying State, verse 17
tells us further, are not permitted to make purchases, and
it is not permitted to buy from them. In other words, they
are boycotted.

In the Roman State emperor worship is the point at
which the State exceeds its proper bounds, at which it
poses as a redemptive institution, so to speak, in order
to rule over even the souls of its subjects. For the rest,
the Roman State was a legitimate State, knowing how to
distinguish between good and evil, as Paul testifies explicitly. Even a legitimate State is always in danger of
becoming satanic in one way or another. We do too great
honor to the German national-socialistic State when we
put it on the same level with the Roman State. So far as
legality is concerned the national-socialistic State had also
fallen away from the order in which every State is placed;
for here the ethical distinction between good and evil,
right and wrong, no longer prevailed: on the contrary,
right was whatever the State required. That was by no
means the case for the Roman State. But emperor worship
was the point where the excess took place, where the fall
from order became especially perceptible. One could
probably avoid this worship if one occupied no official
office or was not in military service. But one had to sub-

mit to it if one was an official or a soldier, and also if one was denounced as an enemy of the State—and this now became a consideration for the Christians.

The first basis for the State's interference was the general suspicion which was directed against the Christians collectively and which in the case of Jesus rested upon ignorance of the Christian attitude toward the State. But now for the first time emperor worship furnished a continual occasion for condemnation. The refusal to offer sacrifice to the image of Caesar and to utter the Kyrios Kaisar had made condemnation to death the compulsory consequence. And every true Christian *had* to refuse this demand, even if, in accordance with the instructions of Jesus and Paul, he was ever so loyal. They would have acted against the teaching of Jesus and of Paul if they had submitted at this point. If the Roman State had had a loyalty-test in any other form than that emperor worship which was blasphemous for the Christians, the Christians would have been able to meet it in good conscience, and much bloodshed would have been avoided. So long as the State demanded a loyalty-test in the form of submission to emperor worship, there could be no peace between Christianity and the State, however loyal the Christians might be as citizens and however humane individual emperors like Trajan, Hadrian, Antoninus, or Marcus Aurelius. At this point the Roman State remained continuously, up to the time of Constantine, a satanic power.

The author of the Johannine Apocalypse saw with astonishing acumen that the satanic element in the Roman

Empire lay in this deification. For this reason in his stir-
ring description he concentrates almost exclusively on
this aspect. On these grounds I believe, too, that we must
relate to this emperor worship the much-discussed number 666 (or according to other good texts, 616) which is
mentioned in the last verse of the chapter. In what immediately precedes, the subject has been the mark which
certifies that the image of Caesar has been worshipped.
Everyone must have the mark which bears the name of
the beast or the number of his name. And then we read:
"Here is wisdom. Let him who has understanding reckon
the number of the beast. It is the number of a man. And
the number is 666." As has been said, some ancient texts
read 616 here, and this number may be just as original.[4]

The riddle was probably known to all the initiate.
The Greek verb which stands here for "reckon"[5] is used
as a terminus technicus for the peculiar method known
as gematria, which consists in taking the numerical value
of every letter and in this way adding up the letters of
a word. The letters were as a matter of fact used as numerical signs: $a = 1$, $\beta = 2$, and so forth. The expression
used here therefore demands of us this sort of reckoning,
and thus there have been an infinite number of explanations from the time of the Church father Irenaeus until
today.[6] For we must at once remark: the possibilities in
the use of this method are almost unlimited. For naturally

---

[4] Thus, Irenaeus, and the Armenian translation.

[5] ψηφίζειν.

[6] See the commentaries mentioned above.

there are just as many possible solutions as there are possibilities for analysing the number 666 or 616 and arrang-
ing it into smaller numbers. So too the number of solutions which are advanced is past reckoning. The most famous is that which takes Kaisar Nero as the arrangement
of letters, the sum of which is 666. But it works also with
Kaisar Romim. Irenaeus had already made two simultaneous proposals: Lateinos (pronounced 'Latinos') or
Teitan (pronounced 'Titan'); the numerical value of both
words being 666.[7] It works also for Trajan and Hadrian.
Apocalyptic sects of every age take special pleasure in
busying themselves with this number; and naturally by
making a few guesses they always succeed in figuring
out the name of a contemporary. Thus, with a few de-
tours, it is possible to find as the basis of the number the
names of Napoleon, Wilhelm the Second, or Hitler.

E. Lohmeyer provides a quite different way.[8] He
shows that by various numerical operations the number
666 can be traced back to the number 8 (one adds the
numbers from 1 to 8, the sum being 36; then one adds the
numbers from 1 to 36, and the sum is 666). But now 8
was the number of the Devil (7 plus 1; therefore the
number which destroys the divine harmony which is designated by 7; just as 13 [12 plus 1] destroys the harmony
which finds expression in the number 12). In spite of the
fact that this interpretation is attractive, the question
must be asked, whether the Greek verb for "reckon" can

---

[7] Irenaeus, *Adv. Haereses*, V, 30:3.
[8] *Die Offenbarung des Johannes*, pp. 115f.

be applied to this numerical operation. As a terminus technicus it appears much rather to designate the method of gematria.

Obviously it will never be possible to say with certainty which of the solutions arrived at in this way is actually the one which the author had in mind and which was recognised with comparative ease by his first readers. But it must possess a plausibility of the highest possible degree. In order to achieve this it is appropriate to give the context the most careful consideration possible. We have seen that the whole paragraph speaks of the worship of the emperor. And now we must take note of the sentence: "It is the number of a man." This does not suit Lohmeyer's interpretation very well. When the author emphasises that it is the number of a man, then it could be that the words hidden in the number contain a *divine* attribute, a title which belongs to God alone and which this man applies to himself in a blasphemous way. In this respect I should be inclined to give preference to A. Deissmann's hypothesis.[9] According to him the designation hidden in the number reads Kaisar Theos: Caesar is God! The numerical value of this confession, which was characteristic of the worship of the emperor, comes to 616. In the formula Kyrios Kaisar or Kaisar Theos the monstrous and satanic claim of the State reveals itself most obviously. Then the amplification, "It is the number of a man," takes on a particularly concrete meaning. The

[9] A. Deissmann, *Licht vom Osten*, 4th ed., 1923, p. 238, n. 3.

Caesar is a human being, and yet he wants to be worshipped as God in the confession he demands of his subjects. Therefore he is presented here as the servant of the dragon, the Devil.

Whether this interpretation of the number is right or not, it is in any case thoroughly suited to the fundamental thought of the whole chapter, which is established even apart from this by the totalitarian religious claim of the State.

Now we understand why we hear a tone quite different here from that in Romans 13. In all other points the Johannine Apocalypse may be a book radically different from the Epistle to the Romans; but in the interpretation of the State there is no contradiction—no more than there is within the Pauline letters themselves or among the sayings of Jesus. Regarding the State's requirement of worship of Caesar's image Paul would not have spoken otherwise than the author of the Johannine Apocalypse. Moreover our present chapter contains a verse which leads us back to Romans 13. In the beginning of the chapter we discover the holy indignation at the blasphemous bearing of the State which deifies itself; yet in verse 10 we read: "If one kills with the sword, by the sword he must die." [10] Here we are reminded of the limitation placed on resistance even to the totalitarian State. We

[10] The text here is of course not certain. According to Codex A, one should translate: "When one is destined to be killed by the sword, then he must be killed by the sword."

must resist the totalitarian demand of this State, and indeed at any cost; but only within the compass of this demand. This means: positively, perseverance in our Christian preaching; negatively, perseverance in our refusal of the idolatry demanded by the State. The totalitarian demand we have to resist even to blood; but it is not our business to take the sword, to wage war as the fellowship of Christians against this State in order to destroy its existence. This is said even by the author of the Johannine Apocalypse, who describes the satanic beast so powerfully. The saying in verse 10 according to the generally admitted reading leads us back also to Jesus, to his decisive renunciation of Zealotism in Gethsemane in the face of his followers' Zealotist pattern of behavior, as we read in Matthew 26:52, "All that take the sword shall perish with the sword."

Before we draw our final conclusion, however, reference must be made to one last saying in the New Testament which speaks of an unreservedly positive relationship between Christians and the State: the prayer for the State and those who stand at its head. This holds true even at the point where the State reveals itself as the beast from the abyss. This positive relationship may never, indeed cannot, be broken. The text to which I refer occurs in the Pastoral Epistles, I Tim. 2:1–2: "I entreat you to offer supplications, prayers, intercessions, and thanksgivings for all men, for kings and all who are in positions of leadership; that we may lead a quiet and peaceable life in all piety and decency." Even in times when the Christians were being most cruelly persecuted by the State this prayer did not cease to be voiced. Because the Christian never renounces the State as an institution, he will always pray for it.

Conclusion

WE HAVE reached the end of our presentation. When one and the same problem is pursued through all the books of the New Testament, ordinarily one is used to finding as his final result the difference in style and method among the different authors as they handle and solve the problem at hand. For the problem of the State matters are exactly reversed. Here we find at the beginning, at the initial point of our investigation, an almost radical difference apparently existing between Romans 13 and Revelation 13; but as the final result there is demonstrated a fundamental unity in the valuation of the State. The apparent contradiction comes on one side from the State itself. According as the State remains within its limits or transgresses them, the Christian will describe it as the servant of God or as the instrument of the Devil.

But further: the apparent contradiction lies in the chronological dualism, the chronological tension, which characterises the New Testament situation. The conviction that the end-time has already begun and that its consummation is nevertheless still outstanding, this tension between "already fulfilled" and "not yet completed" is in no sense a contradiction in the primitive Christian eschatology; rather it is an *essential* part of it. And as long as this primitive Christian tension between "already fulfilled" and "not yet completed" is present, the attitude of the Christians to the State is also uniform. Since this tension is the constitutive element of all primitive Christian interpretation of the end-time, therefore also the apparent contradictions in the primitive Christian interpretation of the State are in reality not contradictions; rather they are rooted in this chronological tension.

Primitive Christian eschatology is not merely a waiting for the future, as Albert Schweitzer and his disciples in Switzerland maintain; but neither is it merely faith in the present as already fulfilled, "realised eschatology," to use C. H. Dodd's expression. It is both. And above all, it is important to me to emphasise that this *tension* between "now" and "one day" did not make its first appearance only as a secondary solution offered by a Christianity already developing toward catholicism. It does not represent a later solution born of embarrassment, as Albert Schweitzer's disciples [11] and Rudolf Bultmann also

[11] See for example F. Buri, *Das Problem der ausgebliebenen Parusie*, *Schweiz. Theol. Umschau*, 1946, pp. 97ff. In answer to Buri's work,

maintain. It is rather, I emphasise, both essentially and from the beginning characteristic of the situation of the New Covenant. That the end-time is expected shortly is nothing new: it is a Jewish hope. What is new is this: that this hope in the future is combined with the faith that the end-time has already begun. And this characteristic connection between present and future is already to be found *in Jesus himself.*[12] On one hand we hear that the Kingdom of God is still expected soon; on the other, Jesus says that he has already seen Satan fall from heaven (Luke 10:18); that "The Kingdom of God has already come upon you" since he "by the Spirit of God casts out demons" (Matt. 12:28). "Go and tell John what you see and hear," he replies when the Baptist's emissaries ask whether he is the one who is coming (that is, who is to come in the future): "The blind see again, the lame walk, lepers are cleansed, the deaf hear, the dead are raised up, and the Gospel is preached to the poor!" (Matt. 11:4f).

The existence of this tension between present and future: this is what is new, what makes its appearance with Jesus. Otherwise we should still be in Judaism. If the hope in the future is more intensive than in Judaism, this is precisely because there is present the conviction that the end-time has already been inaugurated. For the "not yet consummated" is to be emphasised just as strongly as

see O. Cullmann, *Das wahre durch die ausgebliebene Parusie gestellte neutestamentlichen Problem, Theol. Zeitschrift,* 1947, pp. 177ff.
[12] See W. G. Kümmel, *Verheissung und Erfüllung,* 2nd. ed., 1953.

the "already inaugurated." Both together: that is the New Testament.

This is why the New Testament neither affirms nor denies the world. The dualism which we find in the New Testament is a chronological dualism between Now and the Future. It is not the hellenistic dualism between this-worldliness and otherworldliness. Therefore the Christian antithesis does not lead to the ascetic renunciation of present conditions, among which the State belongs in the first rank. It is wrong for one to deduce *only* the negative side from the saying in I Cor. 7:29ff, about the married who are to live as though they were not married, those that weep as if they did not weep, those who rejoice as if they did not rejoice, those who trade as if they possessed nothing. What is said here presupposes also that the Christians are *still* marrying, *still* weeping, *still* rejoicing, *still* trading. In this respect I agree with Amos N. Wilder when he says that the New Testament does not know "otherworldliness." [13] To be sure, however, the other side, the negative, remains in full force.

We have found this same duality also in the attitude toward the State. Indeed the genuine State of the Christians, the "politeuma," is in heaven, as Paul says in Phil. 3:20; but the earthly State is God's servant so long as it remains in the order which is willed by God. The State does not have to be Christian. The Roman State in Rom.

[13] A. N. Wilder, *Otherworldliness and the New Testament*, 1954.

13 was heathen. It can remain in God's present order without itself knowing that it does so, if it remains only State and does not try to be more than State. It possesses a knowledge of good and evil which is given to it even as a heathen State. The Christian, to be sure, knows about the place the State occupies in God's economy of salvation; he knows why the State is able to distinguish between good and evil. Therefore, paradoxical as it may seem, it is precisely the Christian who is able to ascribe a higher dignity to the State—even the heathen State—than the non-Christian citizen can do. To be sure, however, for just this reason the Christian will see his assignment regarding the State in these terms: that he remain in principle critical towards it, and that he watch to see that at no point does the State, whichever it may be, fall away from the divine order. And for the same reason, because on the basis of the Christian revelation he knows of the State's place within the divine order, the Christian will also be more keenly sensitive than any other citizen when a State falls away from God's order. Where others see that a State is becoming "totalitarian" the Christian sees that the powers, subjected by Christ to God's service, are once again breaking loose and becoming satanic. Heathen State and Gospel are therefore thoroughly compatible. Gospel and a totalitarian State in any guise and in any particular point are in principle incompatible.

The Church's task with regard to the State, which is posed for all time, is thus clear. First, it must loyally give the State everything necessary to its existence. It has to

oppose anarchy and all Zealotism within its own ranks.
Second, it has to fulfil the office of watchman over the
State. That means: it must remain in principle critical
toward *every* State and be ready to warn it against trans-
gression of its legitimate limits. Third, it must deny to the
State which exceeds its limits whatever such a State demands that lies within the province of religio-ideological
excess; and in its preaching the Church must courageously
describe this excess as opposition to God.

The Church will fulfil this assignment if it remains
faithful to the fundamental eschatological attitude of the
New Testament. It could be shown how in the course of
history the Church has always assumed a false attitude
toward the State when it has forgotten that the present
time is already fulfilment, but not yet consummation.
Then we get such erroneous solutions as meet us ever and
again in history: either that the Church tries to put itself
in the place of the State: or else that the State is simply
accepted uncritically in all that it does, as if there were
no problem at all. Although the bearing of the Church
in the two cases is radically opposite, in both cases the
Church is guilty of the same fault: relinquishment of the
New Testament interpretation of the end-time.

Just this interpretation is the association of Church
and State in a peaceful and fruitful co-existence.

On the side of the State the stipulation is—not that it
must necessarily be Christian—but indeed that it know
its *limits* (and that it can do so we have heard in the
Epistle to the Romans). Secondly, moreover, that it take

the trouble to *understand* as much of the attitude of its Christian subjects as it is *able* to understand. In this connection the cross of Jesus should serve the State as a warning signal.

EXCURSUS

*On the most recent discussion
of the* ἐξουσίαι *in Romans 13:1* *

---

* First published in *Theologische Zeitschrift*, 1954, pp. 321–336. We wish to re-emphasise the fact that our general understanding of the Pauline conception of the State, as developed in Chapter III, does not stand or fall with our particular interpretation of ἐξουσίαι.

For the past several years a kind of consensus has existed among theologians, especially in Germany, rejecting the interpretation of the ἐξουσίαι of Romans 13:1 according to which the term refers simultaneously to the state and to the angel powers. They reject this interpretation because it presents an exegesis of the passage which, to use some of their own descriptive terms, is altogether 'irrational,' 'eccentric,' 'fantastic,' 'strange' and 'grotesque'! As a result of this consensus, it has been thought possible to write off the interpretation by the simple expedient of hurling an accusing sentence at the theologians who represent it, using the kind of adjectives I have mentioned, and the list could be lengthened! [1]

Martin Dibelius first proposed that the ἐξουσίαι of Romans 13:1 refers both to the State and to the angel powers, in his book, *Die Geisterwelt im Glauben des Paulus* in 1909. But he himself later rejected it when, in 1936 and the years following, Günther Dehn and others pursued it further, and drew implications from this concept for Biblical theology. The fact that this exegesis was developed in research on the State in the

---

[1] In view of the present general diffusion of this consensus it is all the more noteworthy that W. Künneth in his recent large work *Politik zwischen Dämon und Gott* (*Eine Christliche Ethik des Politischen*), 1954 did not follow it, but instead places the question of the political world order in the New Testament within the framework of the Lordship of Christ "over all mights and powers of the invisible dimensions of the cosmic and the historical spheres" (p. 40). Another exception is W. Schweizer, *Die Herrschaft Christi und der Staat im N. T.*, 1949, who, on the whole, follows my view presented in *Königherrschaft Christi und Kirche*, 1941.

New Testament precisely between the years 1936 and 1944,[2] has led various of its opponents simply to charge its appearance to the political events of that period, and thereby to dismiss it. Naturally, the interest in this complex of questions was especially vigorous during that time. But by the same token, one could explain the passionate opposition to the thesis, which also began in Germany during the war years, in the same fashion.[3] However, we seem to have reached the point at which such considerations should once for all disappear from this exegetical debate. The irrelevance of the contemporary political situation for the appearance of this interpretation should be evident simply from the fact that it first appeared in the year 1909.

For this reason I fail to understand a certain heatedness of tone with which even today its opponents mention the so-called 'demonic interpretation' (which is a quite misleading term, incidentally!). When in the title of this essay I spoke of the 'most recent discussion' of the subject, I was employing a euphemism. The 'discussion' is limited for the most part to a summary verdict which is interesting neither to the reader nor to the defeated opponents, since it is not supported by evidence. As an example, I cite here a sentence from Bultmann's review of my book *Christ and Time*,[4] because he is representative of the current consensus and of its methods of procedure: "It is unfortunate that (in *Christ and Time*) the grotesque

[2] For bibliography and for a discussion of those years, see O. Cullmann, *Christ and Time*, 2d ed. 1948, pp. 169ff. On Dibelius' later views, see "Rom und die Christen im 1. Jahrhundert," in *Sitzber. Heidelb. Ak. Wiss.*, 1941–42. See further H. Schlier, "Mächte und Gewalten im N. T.", *Theol. Blätter*, 1930, p. 292.

[3] See especially G. Kittel, *Christus and Imperator*, 1939, pp. 48ff.

[4] R. Bultmann, *Heilsgeschichte und Geschichte. Zu Oscar Cullmann, Christus und die Zeit* (*Theologische Literaturzeitung*, 1948, pp. 659ff).

misinterpretation of Romans 13:1 as referring to the angel powers recurs." Bultmann does not inform us why it is a 'grotesque misinterpretation.'

If in what follows I take up the argument once again, I do it not with the purpose of attempting to establish this interpretation as the only possible one, but rather in the hope that its opponents may take it seriously as an hypothesis quite worthy of consideration when they refer to it in the future, and that they may take the trouble really to oppose it, instead of imperiously dismissing it.

But I also address myself to this question because at least one interpretation has appeared in the postwar period, which constitutes a notable exception to the procedure which we have characterised with the quotation from Bultmann. It really makes a contribution to the discussion, and therefore deserves an answer. I refer to the essay of H. von Campenhausen entitled "On the Exegesis of Romans 13—the demonistic interpretation of the ἐξουσίαι concept," which appeared in 1950 in the memorial volume for A. Bertholet. The Church historian from Heidelberg is equally as decisive in his rejection of the newly investigated thesis as the representatives of the previously mentioned consensus, and one may even detect in his article a certain degree of irritation which is otherwise not characteristic of him. But his objections remain thoroughly relevant, and in some aspects they carry the discussion further.[5] Nor has the author lost his sense of humor, which is illustrated when, for the sake of simplicity, he calls the representatives of the interpretation which he opposes 'the demonists'!

Of course, this term as well as the slightly qualified term

---

[5] Especially thought provoking are the patristic supplementations, above all the reference to Origen, p. 102, which, to be sure, does not speak against the thesis which H. von Campenhausen disputes.

'demonistic interpretation,' invites misunderstanding from the very beginning. For it is characteristic of the exegesis which I together with others defend, that it does not onesidedly relate the ἐξουσίαι to the angel powers alone, but to both: to the empirical State *and* to the angel powers. Moreover, H. von Campenhausen has correctly recognised this fact. Again in this point he is a notable exception in the treatment of the question, in that he does not over-simplify the opposing view, but represents it accurately.

The agitation over the suggested interpretation is also difficult for me to understand because it by no means introduces a radically new understanding of the Pauline conception of the State in Romans 13:1ff, as opposed to the usual interpretation considered apart from the question of the meaning of the ἐξουσίαι. On the contrary, this interpretation only places the 'powers' within the theological context of the total Pauline thought, and thus proposes to add a dimension of depth to the understanding of them. In the final analysis H. von Campenhausen gives exactly the same theological interpretation to the total passage as I—in spite of his energetic rejection of the two-fold interpretation of ἐξουσίαι. I could subscribe word for word to what he says on page 107—not *in spite of* my understanding of the ἐξουσίαι, but *because* of it. He refers to the fact that for Paul the subjection of the Christian to the civil authorities is based on eschatology; and that it is therefore no accident that the 13th chapter of Romans closes with a portrayal of the great and imminent future consummation of Christ and his kingdom, from which point everything is understood: 'the night is far spent.' H. von Campenhausen continues in these words: ". . . with this, in a few words, the impressively emphasised weight of authority becomes clear in all its provisionality and limitedness. Civil governments are yet-existing but fading powers, on which the Christian is de-

pendent for the present time, but there is no point in arguing
about their individual justness or unjustness." [6] I agree whole-
heartedly with this. The author here sees the Pauline explanation of the State not as based in some way on natural law, but
on *Heilsgeschichte*. It is therefore not true when he insists that
the interpretation which I among others defend 'does not fit
the clearly recognizable purpose which Paul is pursuing in this
passage.'

On the contrary, by this two-fold relatedness of the
ἐξουσίαι, the eschatological orientation of our passage, which
the Heidelberg historian stresses, and which is evident from
the context no matter how one interprets the ἐξουσίαι, is confirmed, both from the standpoint of philology and of the
Jewish concepts. By means of this interpretation, one sees
especially how the concept of the provisionality of the State
is clothed in the Pauline *heilsgeschichtliche* categories which
the apostle shared with his time, as did all of Christendom.
Therefore it is difficult to see why the rejection of our interpretation follows; and indeed a rather passionate rejection, as
if by the two-fold interpretation of the ἐξουσίαι the greatest
violence had been done to Paul, and as if his concept of the
State had been completely distorted! [7]

[6] On the other hand, the argument of H. von Campenhausen on pages
109ff seems to me to be weak, where he writes concerning the parallel
between our passage in Romans and 1 Thess. 5:1–15, to which he
apparently attributes a special significance. Certainly the use of figures
is parallel. But one may not set the leaders of the congregation in
parallel to the civil authorities. Obedience to the leaders of the congregation does not have to be established with reference to the escha-
ton. Obedience to the State has to be laid especially on the hearts of
the members of the congregation, because it is not self-explanatory.
Obviously Paul must also promote obedience to the προιστάμενοι, but
he does not have to justify it!

[7] H. von Campenhausen also speaks of 'confusion,' 'tortuous exegetical
tricks.' Similarly, G. Bornkamm, *Das Ende des Gesetzes*, 1952, p. 169.

But what is the status, then, of this two-fold interpretation? H. von Campenhausen has correctly noted that the word ἐξουσίαι has only one meaning in secular Greek: it refers to the empirical civil authorities. The conception of angel powers is certainly unknown in that sphere! [8] This fact also has meaning for me. If in Romans 13 we had to do with a secular Greek text, then obviously it would be necessary to assume only the meaning 'civil State' for ἐξουσίαι. However, Romans 13 does not belong in a secular Greek context, but in a Jewish-hellenistic context, and indeed a theological, or more precisely, a Pauline one. In this context the word ἐξουσίαι definitely has a two-fold meaning. Not only was the meaning 'angel powers' *current* to the early Christian reader, but we may say even more. For Paul, in any case, the plural ἐξουσίαι and the plurally-used singular πᾶσα ἐξουσία mean in every other instance *only* 'invisible powers.' When H. von Campenhausen writes (on page 99), "Paul *also* uses the word ἐξουσίαι to mean certain angels in other contexts," [9] this is certainly not false, but it is nevertheless misleading. No, we may *not* say that Paul *also* uses the word ἐξουσίαι to refer to certain angels; but we may say that he *does* use it in all other passages throughout *only* in this sense, as the concordance shows. This may be accidental, but at least it indicates why I insist that the meaning 'angel powers' for ἐξουσίαι is to be taken into consideration in a Pauline epistle, not only for the writer but for his first-century readers as well. At least it indicates why I do not consider my insistence on this position to be so 'grotesque' as it has been repeatedly deemed! Certainly the secular sense was

---

[8] But I would quickly add that also the ἄρχοντες of 1 Cor. 2:8, of whom it is said that they crucified Christ, meant nothing more to a secular reader than 'empirical rulers.' We will see that H. von Campenhausen, on the contrary, now wishes to understand the ἄρχοντες only in the sense of 'demonic powers'! (see below pp. 106f).

[9] Italics mine.

also known to the Apostle. How could it have been otherwise!
It is equally certain that here in this passage he *also* had this
secular sense in mind: that is, the 'civil authorities,' which the
entire context indicates.[10]

I do not know what scientific principle H. von Campenhausen is using as a basis when he sets up the rule that we
must 'normally' understand the ἐξουσίαι in a case like Romans
13 as it can be understood only in a purely secular context. It
is as though the Apostle had here suddenly ceased to speak
as a theologian! [11] If Paul's use of the term ἐξουσίαι in the sense
of angel powers were only an occasional, peripheral phe-
nomenon, then one might well say that only the secular meaning 'civil authorities' could come into consideration, although
there is no other example of such a use in the Pauline epistles.

Apart from these word-statistics, however, the concept of
the angel powers and of their subjection by Christ stands quite
in the foreground, not only of Pauline thought, but of the
thought of the earliest Christian Church as well. In almost
every case these powers appear in the primitive confessional
formulas of the Church, although these formulas are charac-

[10] And again I add: in the same way he also takes into account in 1 Cor.
2:8 that in secular Greek ἄρχοντες are earthly rulers, and in the same
way there the context indicates that Paul also had in mind rulers of
flesh and blood, when it speaks of the Roman death penalty of crucifixion.

Accordingly I am not at all so certain that the gnostics cited by
Irenaeus (*Adv. Haer.* V 24:1) could not have been thinking about the
State. The fact that Irenaeus speaks only of the "angelicis potestatibus"
and "invisibilibus principibus" in his representation of their ideas does
not yet constitute confirmation to the contrary. One has only to compare the way in which most of the opponents of our interpretation
characterise it, as if the ἐξουσίαι were to be related *only* to the angel
powers. (Cf. above!)

It is correct to say, on the other hand, that these gnostics nevertheless misinterpreted Paul, insofar as they appear to have understood the
angel powers only in malam partem.
[11] See below (p. 104) in this connection.

teristically brief, introducing only the most germane elements. I would like to draw special attention to this argument, because it seems to me to be decisive for this question in Romans 13: "Can Paul have had in mind another meaning for ἐξουσίαι alongside the secular Greek sense of 'civil authorities,' even though he is using the expression within the framework of a discourse concerning the state?"

Nothing shows more clearly how the concept of the present Lordship of Christ and also of his consequent victory over the angel powers stands at the very center of early Christian thought than the frequent citation of Psalm 110, not only in isolated books, but in the entire New Testament. There is no other Old Testament passage which is so often cited by all New Testament authors as this one.[12] The affirmation that Jesus is seated at the right hand of God in fulfillment of the words of the Psalm is only another means of expressing the earliest creed: 'Kyrios Christos'—'Christ is Lord.' This became so current that it was repeated completely apart from any reference to the Old Testament Psalm. Nevertheless, the recollection of its original connection with the Psalm did not die out, because it became typical that the session at the right hand of God and the victory over the angel powers were mentioned simultaneously.[13] This clearly stems from Psalm 110, where it is declared that the Lord shall sit at the right hand of God until his enemies are made his footstool. While it is true that the Old Testament Psalm here refers to the earthly enemies of Israel, the first Christians identified the 'enemies'

---

[12] Rom. 8:34; 1 Cor. 15:25; Col. 3:1; Eph. 1:20; Hebr. 1:3; 8:1; 10:13; 1 Pet. 3:22; Acts 2:34; 5:31; 7:55; Rev. 3:21; Matt. 22:44; 26:64; Mark 12:36; 14:62; 16:19; Luke 20:42; 22:69. We also confront this citation in the apostolic fathers: 1 Clem. 36:5; Barn. 12:10.

[13] So Eph. 1:20 καθίσας ἐν δεξιᾷ αὐτρῦ ἐν τοῖς οὐρανοῖς ὑπεράνω πάσης ἀρχῆς καὶ ἐξουσίας etc. See especially the confessional texts cited in what follows.

with the invisible powers. Their subjection bears testimony
that now Christ alone is Lord. Even though the powers con-
tinue to exist, they are stripped of all independent authority.

The importance of this faith for early Christianity becomes
evident from the fact that the assertion recurs with an astound-
ing frequency in the old confessional formulas which are ex-
tant even in the New Testament, and among the earliest
Church fathers, that Christ sits at the right hand of God, with
all 'powers' subject to him.[14] Consider 1 Peter 3:22, where an
ancient confessional formula may unmistakeably be distin-
guished from the context: ". . . (he) has gone into heaven,
and is at the right hand of God, with angels, authorities and
powers ($\dot{\epsilon}\xi o v\sigma \acute{\iota}\alpha\iota$) subject to him." To cite a further example:
the important Christological confession in Philippians 2:6
reaches its climax in the belief in the subordination of the
$\dot{\epsilon}\pi o v\rho \acute{\alpha}\nu\iota\alpha$, the $\dot{\epsilon}\pi \acute{\iota}\gamma\epsilon\iota\alpha$ and the $\kappa\alpha\tau\alpha\chi\theta \acute{o}\nu\iota\alpha$—'those in heaven, those
on earth, and those under the earth.' These are the ones in
this passage whose 'knees shall bow' before Christ, and whose
'tongues shall confess' that Jesus is Lord. In the formula from
1 Timothy 3:16 we read that Christ was 'seen by angels.'
Outside of the New Testament, the subjection of these powers
is expressly mentioned in the formula cited by Ignatius of
Antioch and by Polycarp (Trallians 9:1; the Letter of Polycarp 2:1). Again, in Irenaeus we establish the fact that the
confession of Christ as Lord is a confession of his lordship
over all powers of the whole creation, both visible and invisible (*Adv. Haer.* 1:10, 1).

In the light of this evidence, it is clear that we are not
dealing here with a peripheral assertion, but with an altogether central article of faith, which first disappeared from the
confessions of the ancient Church when the concept of the

---

[14] See in relation to this O. Cullmann, *Die ersten christlichen Glaubens-
bekenntnisse*, 2d ed. 1949, pp. 53ff.

angel powers was no longer current, leaving as a remnant of
the old affirmation only the first part: the 'session at the right
hand of God.'

The great importance of this belief in the subjection of
the angel powers in the earliest times is evident from the fact
that Paul himself mentions them in so central a passage as
1 Corinthians 15:25, where he states that they will be subjected. In Colossians 1:20 and 2:15 Paul says that through the
cross they have *already* been subjected. Later on we will have
more to say concerning this temporal tension between past
and future.

From the point of view of this evidence we must then
ask: When Paul uses the word ἐξουσίαι in Romans 13:1, can
we assume that he has forgotten the meaning of the word
which so decisively controlled his own theological thinking
and that of his readers? One may object that it is irrelevant to
postulate this whole theological-Christological background in
the treatment of so concrete a question as that of the conduct
of the Christian in relation to the State; that this would only
be relevant in a dogmatic or mythological context. But in what
passage has Paul set out to answer a concrete question of individual or social ethics without placing it within the Christo-
logical-heilsgeschichtliche framework of his whole theology?
In what passage has he spoken from a purely secular standpoint concerning such a matter? Certainly Paul was not aware
of the modern distinction between two separate spheres of
life—one secular and the other sacred. I mentioned earlier the
correct judgment of H. von Campenhausen that everything
said here about the State is said on the basis of eschatology.
But for early Christian thought, it was impossible to separate
the relationship between eschatology and the present, which
is here in question, from the concept of the victory of Christ

over the angel powers—a victory that is already won, but which is not yet consummated.

At this point H. von Campenhausen raises an objection which also hinders many others from accepting the interpretation of the ἐξουσίαι of Romans 13 which includes the concept of the angel powers as well as the empirical State in the understanding of the term. He objects that if this concept of the angel powers had been intended by Paul, it surely would have been so explained and elaborated in the context. In and for itself this objection is justified. This is precisely the reason for my strong emphasis upon the central place in all early Christianity occupied by the specifically primitive Christian belief in the subjection of the powers, as something which has already been accomplished, but which is not yet consummated. So he can refer to it without mentioning it explicitly. Outside of the passage in question, there are many things relating to this belief which appear in the letters of Paul as tacit presuppositions, and are never once explained. For example, it is certain that the different expressions which Paul used to designate the various powers were not synonymous for him. Yet in none of the epistles does he describe the special function of a single one of the so-designated powers. What do we learn from Paul concerning the στοιχεῖα τοῦ κόσμου ('the elemental spirits of the universe'), in Galatians 4:3, 9, for example, where incidentally this expression is used in connection with rather concrete questions? The manner in which the 'elemental spirits' are related to these concrete situations is nowhere explained.

H. von Campenhausen has postulated that the ἐξουσίαι in Romans 13:1 must be understood in a different sense than that which the word conveys in all other Pauline passages. It occurs to me that in the final analysis, this postulate results for the Germans from the traditional translation of Luther which is so familiar throughout the German-speaking world, "Let every man be subject to the Obrigkeit." [15] If we translate with a closer dependence upon the Greek text: "let every man be subject to the powers," then the richly-varied depth of the word becomes clear at once, even in this passage where, of course, the State is under discussion. When one so quickly rejects the thought of a relationship between angel powers and civil governments, is not the basic difficulty that which besets one when he attempts to think in late-Jewish and early Christian categories? This belief in subjected angel powers is far removed from us in this demythologising age, and in fact, even in ancient Christendom the reference to such powers soon vanished from the creed.

H. von Campenhausen does not deny that Paul believed in this victory of Christ over the angel powers, but he does deny that Paul conceived of a connection between the angel powers and the civil authorities, since he contends that there is no documentation for such a view in the Pauline works. He refuses to consider my reference to 1 Corinthians 2:8 as such a documentation, where Paul speaks of the ἄρχοντες τοῦ αἰῶνος τούτου—'the rulers of this age'—who, without being aware of what they were doing, crucified the Lord of Glory. Again, H. von Campenhausen rejects the idea that the word ἄρχοντες, 'rulers,' could include both the empirical, human rulers and the invisible powers. But here, strangely enough, it is only the 'demonic' or mythological meaning which he wishes to allow, exactly reversing his position on Romans 13:1, where he recognises only the empirical sense. In spite of the different contexts, however, the two usages are quite analogous. In

---

[15] Also the following words: "which has power over him" are not entirely correct from the standpoint of the Greek text.

secular Greek ἄρχοντες meant nothing for the non-Jewish and
non-Christian reader except 'earthly rulers.' Using the same
argument by which H. von Campenhausen rejects the relationship of the ἐξουσίαι in Romans 13 to invisible powers, one
could reject the interpretation of the ἄρχοντες as referring to
demonic rulers, the only interpretation which he recognises.
Indeed, such a rejection of his position concerning 1 Cor. 2:8
on this ground has recently been made.

As evidence for the purely demonic character of the
'rulers' in 1 Corinthians 2:8, H. von Campenhausen refers to
what he calls the 'whole mythical imagery' of the context.[16]
Nevertheless, the passage also refers to something which is
very concrete, something which took place in an altogether
empirical, historical framework—namely, the crucifixion of
Jesus, the execution upon him of the Roman death penalty.
How is it possible to think only of demons as the agents of this
historical event? It is no mere coincidence that just as many
cogent grounds have been presented for relating the ἄρχοντες
of 1 Corinthians 2:8 to Pilate and Herod as may be presented
for relating them to demonic elements.[17] J. Schniewind has
been the most recent and most energetic representative of the
empirical, historical interpretation of 1 Corinthians 2:8 as the
only possible one.[18] His arguments seem to me to be just as
valid as those of exegetes such as H. von Campenhausen, who
choose to think here only of the demonic powers. They are
just as valid, but on the other hand, just as erroneous in their

---

[16] P. 100. In the case of Rev. 12 which he cites as parallel, the historical
relationship is even more equivocal.

[17] The clear parallel in Acts 3:17 (οἶδα ὅτι κατὰ ἄγνοιαν ἐπράξατε ὥσπερ
καὶ οἱ ἄρχοντες ὑμῶν) shows that earthly ἄρχοντες also must be included
in the idea, as does Acts 13:27f.

[18] J. Schniewind, *Nachgelassene Reden und Aufsätze*, 1952, pp. 104ff.
("Die Archonten dieses Aeons").

one-sidedness. We are not dealing here with an Either/Or, but with a Both/And—both with the angel powers and with their earthly agents.

H. von Campenhausen simply fails to mention 1 Corinthians 6:1ff, a passage which is extremely important for our question. This passage demonstrates the very eschatological temporariness of all subjection to the State, an idea which he himself emphasises in the New Testament. The members of the Christian congregation are instructed to keep themselves aloof from the civil courts in their legal quarrels, in spite of the fact that according to Romans 13:1 the heathen State is able to distinguish between good and evil. It is the reason for this attitude toward the civil courts given in 1 Corinthians 6:3 which is especially interesting to us here. The verse bases this attitude on the ground that the Christians are to judge the ἄγγελοι. But why should this remarkable reason have been given? Paul might have been content simply to write that the Christian would one day take part in the last Judgment! Why then does he speak of a judgment over the angels? If the angels were not expressly mentioned here, someone would certainly object that it would be 'grotesque' to assume that for Paul the angels should have anything to do with the treatment of so concrete a question as process before a civil court. We must seriously ask ourselves whether also in this passage the concept does not appear, according to which the civil authorities are the executive agents of the angel powers.

Now I would like to move to yet another consideration which further suggests the double meaning of the ἐξουσίαι of Romans 13:1. Early Christianity and late Judaism shared the belief that invisible powers are at work behind all earthly phenomena. The στοιχεῖα τοῦ κόσμου must be understood in this sense. They *are* thought of as cosmic, almost personified powers which direct the on-going course of the universe. On

the other hand, according to Acts 12:15, every man has his
own angel, a belief which Jesus appears to have shared in
Matthew 18:10. Ephesians 6:12 presents the concept that we
fight not against flesh and blood (one should certainly add,
not *only*), but against principalities and powers (ἐξουσίαι),
and the like. According to 1 Corinthians 4:9 the apostles have
'become a spectacle to angels and men.' In Revelation 2 and 3
the churches have their angels.

At this point the late Jewish concept of the angels of the
nations enters the question with special significance. A separate article would have to be written to show how important
this belief in national angels is for late-Jewish thought, as
witnessed especially in the book of Daniel and the books of
Enoch. H. von Campenhausen rejects this consideration, however, on the ground that the belief in national angels is nowhere to be found in Christian sources. But we have already
observed that Paul, or for that matter the whole New Testament, remains silent concerning the individual functions of the
various invisible powers which he so often mentions, and yet
we must assume that he associated a concrete thought with
each different designation which he gives to these powers.
Where may we expect to find further information on the
subject if not in late Judaism? Again, it is impossible to see
what scientific principle rules out this clearly attested late-
Jewish concept of the national angels as admissible documentation. In this connection, the evidence weighs heavily that
just this simultaneous use of the same word for demonic and
earthly rulers is attested in Jewish sources. The same word,
śar, designates kings, earthly rulers, and the invisible rulers as
well.

Is it altogether true, however, that the concept of invisible
rulers governing the earthly kingdoms of the world never
appears in the New Testament? Let us lay aside 1 Corinthians

2:8 for the moment. Apart from this passage, which for me at any rate possesses great evidential value in this question, we find at least an analogous view presupposed in the temptation story according to the synoptic gospels. Here the devil has the ἐξουσία, the authority, over the kingdoms of the world; he has them at his disposal, and therefore can offer them to Jesus.

But according to H. von Campenhausen, the angel powers may not be understood in a double role: that is, in a 'good' role insofar as they have already been subjected since the death and resurrection of Christ; and in an 'evil' role insofar as the drive toward emancipation from this subjection and consequently toward their original demonic independence always remains. For late-Jewish angelology, however, this double role is typical. In the New Testament the singular ἐξουσία (that is, the abstract sense), is used to refer equally to the divine authority as well as to the satanic.[19] But ἐξουσία also designates both the abstract authority and the agents which execute it. This is the case in the earthly sphere.[20] But in the same way the invisible ἐξουσία of God as well as that of the devil must be understood as designating at the same time both the abstract authority and the invisible, but personally conceived agents of this authority. One can see, then, that from the very beginning it is difficult to say whether these powers are good or evil. The late Jewish doctrine of the Fall of the angels hints at this uncertainty and represents an attempt to clarify it in part. Now this same double character of the powers appears in Christian sources more clearly than ever, although in a different manner, and it is positively normative for all New Testament thinking. It appears in connection with what I have

---

[19] The divine: Acts 1:7; Jude 25; Mark 1:22; Matt. 7:29; Mark 2:10; Matt. 21:23; 28:18; the satanic: Luke 22:53; Eph. 2:2.

[20] See in this connection my article "Autorités" in *Vocabulaire biblique,* publié sous la direction de J. J. von Allmen, 1954, p. 28.

called the temporal tension between present and future. The thing which I set out to show in my book *Christ and Time* concerning this tension for the whole New Testament finds its confirmation precisely in this point.

We have seen that in 1 Peter 3:22 the defeat of the powers has already been accomplished, as also in Colossians 1:16ff, 2:15, and in Philippians 2:10. In 1 Corinthians 15:24f and Hebrews 10:13, on the other hand, this defeat is yet to come.[21] The powers have been defeated, and yet they must be defeated again. Both were insisted upon by the first Christians. Did they have any ideas concerning a combination of the two assertions? Certainly the author of the book of Revelation did. He sees the explanation in the temporary binding of Satan, in application, of course, to the millenial kingdom. Is it not natural to assume that the first Christians also reflected about the lot of the already defeated and yet still to be defeated powers? And here emerges the idea of a subjection-in-service under the Lordship of Christ.

It must be conceded to H. von Campenhausen and E. Brunner [22] that we have no text in the New Testament where it is explicitly said that the defeated powers are subjected in service, as we must presuppose in Romans 13:1 if ἐξουσίαι refers to the State and to the angel powers standing behind it as well. On the other hand it is not true that the 'powers' in the New Testament are always enemy powers, as H. von Campenhausen insists. The heavenly, terrestrial and subterranean beings of Philippians 2:10 are no other than angel powers, according to Colossians 1:16.[23] We hear of them that

---

[21] Also the verb καταργέω in the New Testament shares in this temporal tension, so that one must translate 2 Timothy 1:10 with Luther: "he stripped it of its power." Usually it is translated "abolished."

[22] See *Kirchenblatt für die reformierte Schweiz,* 1934, pp. 2ff; 18ff; 34ff, and my reply in *Christus und die Zeit,* pp. 183ff.

[23] Here the identity is clearly expressed.

they bow their knees and confess that Christ is Lord. In Ephesians 3:10 they appear under the designation ἐξουσίαι as objects of revelation. Could it be that this revelation accomplishes only their destruction?

The occurrence of the expression λειτουργικὰ πνεύματα in Hebrews 1:14 is decisive, however. In the context the 'servant spirits' are designated as ἄγγελοι. But in the previous verse Psalm 110 is cited, and here the ἐχθροί (the 'enemies') are mentioned, which are to be made the footstool of the victor. We have seen how current the conception is in the New Testament and also precisely in Hebrews that the ἐχθροί are to be equated with the angel powers. H. von Campenhausen writes that I have fallen into an unusual error on this point, because the λειτουργικὰ πνεύματα of Hebrew 1:14 are, in his own words, "certainly not the previously mentioned ἐχθροί." [24] Is this really so completely out of the question? After I have so confirmed the hardly deniable fact that the early Christian exegesis regularly related the ἐχθροί of Psalm 110 to the subjected angels, it is certainly more than obvious that in this framework, where the angels are spoken of directly in connection with Psalm 110 and the expressly named ἐχθροί, the λειτουργικὰ πνεύματα are the subjugated angels. By this fact is demonstrated the supremacy of the Son over the angels.

Finally, I should like to offer the following for consideration against the objection that a subjection in service of the former enemy nowhere comes into account in the New Testament: If in the oldest confessions the 'session at the right hand of God' is affirmed together with the mention of the defeated powers, does not the question arise: What other meaning could the defeated angel powers have for the Christ exalted

[24] P. 106. I admit, however, that this interpretation which I represent and which in *Christ and Time*, p. 181, is only mentioned, needs a brief clarification on this point.

to the right hand of God—that is, for the Lord exercising his sovereignty—except that they are his servants?

At the beginning of this discussion I remarked that the two-fold interpretation of the ἐξουσίαι does not introduce a radically new concept into the Pauline understanding of the State as it is reflected in the whole passage Romans 13:1ff, and as it is set in the framework of eschatology, which H. von Campenhausen himself correctly does.

But one may ask whether this is not a rather useless hypothesis. We must answer no, because only in this way can the double character of the State be established within the Pauline, and beyond Paul the early Christian concept of the tension between past and future—between the already-accomplished and the not-yet-consummated. Only in this way can we see in Pauline perspective the simultaneousness of the thoroughly positive role of the State on the one hand, and its provisional, in the last analysis problematical character on the other. This is roughly the simultaneousness of Romans 13:1ff and 1 Corinthians 6:1ff. This apparently contradictory situation belongs essentially to the victory over the angel powers, and it becomes graspable, so to speak, in this point. H. von Campenhausen has correctly noted that one may find texts in Judaistic literature that are analogous to Romans 13:1ff. But nowhere does one find there the tension between past and future which is characteristic for Christianity. Nowhere are those positive evaluations of the State which one finds in Judaism furnished with a final question mark of provisionality, as is the case in Christian sources.

The two-fold interpretation of the ἐξουσίαι can perform yet another service: the coincidence of the judgment of the secular State concerning good and evil with the ethical judgment of the Christian, of which the passage Romans 13:1ff speaks, may not be explained by means of eschatology alone. If one wishes to place this within the framework of Pauline theology, one may only do so on the basis of a theory of natural law— something for which it is difficult to find evidence in Paul. If we accept the relationship of the ἐξουσίαι to the angel powers as well as to the secular State, we see how the State, without knowing it, can be the servant of God, and this fact is then based on Christology. For this reason one should speak rather of a Christological interpretation than of a 'demonic' one. According to Colossians 1:16 the angel powers are already 'in Christ,' and consequently also destined for subjection to him. According to the primitive Christian credo they are subjected by Christ. If this is the case, then the whole sphere of invisible powers, including the secular State with them, comes under the Lordship of Christ. This is then a Lordship over the Church and over the State at the same time.[25] This explains, in connection with a central early Christian doctrine (namely, the Lordship of Christ over the powers), how it is possible for secular States to be servants of God, and to be capable of passing a proper judgment of good and evil.

We may now conclude: the two-fold interpretation of the ἐξουσίαι of Romans 13:1 as referring to the State and to the angel powers which stand behind it is thoroughly justified as an hypothesis, from the standpoint of philology, Judaistic concepts and the early Christian and Pauline theology. It is an hypothesis, and naturally we can never say with final certainty that Paul had in mind not only the secular sense of the word ἐξουσίαι, but also the meaning which he himself attributes to it in all other passages. I can only wish, however, that all other hypotheses which we necessarily must use in the field of New Testament science were as well grounded as this one.

[25] I refer the reader here to my illustration of the two concentric circles. See *Christus und die Zeit*, p. 166, and *"Königsherrschaft Christi und Kirche im Neuen Testament,"* 3d ed. 1950.

INDICES

Index of Authors

The numbers in parenthesis refer to the footnotes

Index of Authors 119

Biblical Index

120